Boltik

Author: Vladislav Krapivin (c)

Translator into English: Alexander Koryagin (c) 2016

Illustrations: NC (c)

Contents

Vladislav Krapivin

BOLTIK

Translated by Alexander Koryagin

PREFACE

We, in Russia, like to add the following letters "ik" to a word, to define our tender feelings towards things or names. For instance, Slava is formal, but his grandmother can call him Slavik, denoting her love. Another example — we also have the word "bolt", meaning a piece of metal hardware for fastening two pieces of metal together. There is nothing special in it for an adult. But when a small boy finds a nice, sparkling bolt, he may be really happy. Especially a boy from the 1970s, a time when children had far fewer toys than now and played using their imagination, not ready-to-use computer games. So, when the young hero of this novel found a beautiful, shiny, little bolt, he called it "boltik."

The second name of the novel's young hero is "Rybkin." It is quite funny in Russian. "Ryba" is a fish, "rybka" is a small fish, and the name "Rybkin" underlines the young age of the boy and the kind humor of this story.

The author of this novel is Vladislav Krapivin, the famous Russian writer. In general, his novels are written for children, but many adults find them moving and fascinating. They treasure them with great love. This novel is very original. As a rule, authors describe events that can last for a long period of time, maybe years or even decades. But all the events of this novel occur during just one day. It makes this book quite unique, because only a talented author could write a lengthy novel from such a small timescale. Also he understands that though a child may be small, a child's soul is not small and there is therefore much to write about. You will see how a timid boy became transformed into a new person. And this new life began after he found the *boltik* and went on to sing a song that inspired him and helped him overcome his lack of courage.

You may ask me what is so special in the way Krapivin writes his novels. It is not easy to explain. Perhaps the answer is that they are simply wonderful stories! In this book there is something that you cannot find elsewhere, because that time has long gone, together with the country that was called the USSR. The Russian people tried then to build a kind of idealistic society and, probably, some of their children were even more idealistic than their parents in this new society. I believe it will be interesting to read this story today, like going on a trip to a far off country. A picture may have been painted long ago, but people can still continue admiring it, because they find that the picture is inspiring them even now. "Boltik" is a picture where you can see a child's entire soul, down to the very depths. And the author's talent makes this picture unique, bright, warm and colorful.

Besides that, there is another point here. Most teachers in the USSR thought that children should be brought up to be quiet and obedient, not daring to say a challenging word to adults or to a teacher. But Krapivin always wanted them to be brave, independent and honest, possessing dignity and a desire to fight for it. "Perestroika" (the name of the time when Russia changed dramatically), which approached ahead of that time, needed such people desperately and waited for just such personalities to arrive. When we read the book we see a wonderful event — the birth of the personality within the boy. Such a birth is as important as a physical one, and we are present at the dramatic moment it occurs in Maxim's life.

I express my deep gratitude to Mr. Everett Hertenstein from Nashville, Tennessee, Heather Wright from Scotland

and, of course, to NC.

For those wishing to know how to pronounce two Russian names in the story and the author's name, which all differ from normal English pronunciation, here is a guide: Vladislav Krapivin, Vladik and Maxim. The letter "i" in these names has the same sound when pronounced, as the letter "e" in the word "she".

gAlexKo@gmail.com is my e-mail. Any comments are very welcome.

Facebook: www.facebook.com/BoltikEng

Sincerely yours, Alexander

Chapter one

FIELD CAP

"What a terrible, naughty child," said Mama in despair. "You'll drive me to a heart attack and catch a deadly cold yourself."

The "terrible, naughty child", third grader[1] Maxim Rybkin, huffed angrily at the door next to the shoe shelf. He was fastening his new sandals.

His elder brother, tenth grader Andrew, lounged about the big mirror: he was grooming his mane-like hair with Mama's hairbrush. He said reassuringly:

"Well, he'll hardly manage to catch a deadly cold. Maybe he'll get a bit sniffly and sneeze, but he'll survive, surely."

"It's a madhouse, not a family," said Mama. "The one can't be dragged to a barber, the other does everything

---

[1] *Maxim was nine years old. The school education in the USSR consisted of ten grades. (—Tr.)*

possible to get pneumonia— Igor! You say something, too!"

Papa leaned out from his room. In one hand he held a screwdriver and in the other his electric razor that smelled badly of burnt insulation. One side of Papa's face was shiny and smooth, and the bristles on the other side sparkled in the light of the corridor lamp. Papa wanted to know what had happened.

"What happened?" said Mama. "Our dear son wants to leave the house undressed. And the temperature outside is just seven[1] degrees!"

Maxim coped at last with the buckles on his sandals and straightened up.

"It was seven degrees at six o'clock. And now it's warmer."

"You will be the death of me," said Mama resignedly.

"Maxim," Papa said instructively, "you are a future man and you shouldn't argue with women."

"But if I put this uniform in the bag it'll get creased, and I'll look as if I was pulled out of a hippopotamus' mouth!"

"Oh, what a refined speech! And this is the son of cultured parents? Igor, what are you smiling at? By the way, when there is no consensus between the parents their children become lawbreakers."

"It means that I am almost a complete lawbreaker," said Andrew cheerfully.

"At least outwardly," said Mama. "You look like a long-haired gangster from Chicago."

"Well, I think you are right," agreed Andrew condescendingly.

"Leave my hair brush alone!" ordered Mama and turned to Maxim again: "I am sure that all the children will go to the studio in coats or jackets."

"No, they won't. And if they do, it's not important for them. They stay in their row and nobody will see they are crumpled. And I am in front of them, in front of the mi... crophone."

The last words Maxim said in very low voice, as he

---

[1] 7C or 44F (—Tr.)

took a glance at his brother.

Andrew stood with his back to Maxim and looked at him mischievously through the mirror as though he was going to say, "Guys, leave our soloist alone! He mustn't be nervous, or at the most important moment he'll sing a note 'C' instead of 'B.'" Thankfully, he said nothing, only chuckled. Maxim hurriedly said to his parents:

"You yourselves will say what a slob I am when you see my clothes creased on the television."

"There is some logic in that," noticed Papa.

"It's useless talking to all of you," said Mama. "Let him go naked if he wants. He's not a child, but a little barbarian."

Andrew came away from the mirror, at last, and Maxim slid into his place.

No, he was not a barbarian at all! Barbarians are shaggy, dirty and frightful like pirates. And he was quite a good-looking person. Really good-looking, especially in his new uniform.

The uniform was dark-red, or cherry-colored to be more exact. The little waistcoat, with brass buttons was tight at the waist and loose on the shoulders, keeping the white shirtsleeves and collar visible. The uniform's shorts were ironed so well that their creases jutted out like little axes (and Maxim's legs resembled the axe handles; they were still untanned and light as though they were made of fresh chipped wood). On his feet he wore a pair of red sandals. The anklets were red too. It was the new uniform for the children's ensemble. And the sandals were bought by Mama because Maxim would be standing in front of the chorus, and everything on him should be as neat as a pin.

Now everything looked as it should. The field cap was best of all. It was cherry-colored too, made of thin cloth with white edging and silver wings embroidered on the left side, because the junior chorus group in the ensemble was called "The Little Wings."

Together the two chorus groups, two orchestras and a dance group had a very long name which was difficult to remember: "Chkalov Culture Palace's Children's Musical Choreographic Ensemble[1]."

The palace was originally built for pilots. They say that long ago at that place was the town's main airfield. When jet planes appeared, the airfield was too small for them. The new airport was built far beyond the town, and at the old place there remained just a small landing field for small planes and helicopters.

The regional flight-control administration also preserved their place. The Palace of Culture was located near it.

Maxim's father was not a pilot; he was an engineer at a large building firm. And his mother was head teacher at the Arts School. Regardless of that the ensemble enrolled not only the pilots' children. Where could you find so many of them? Every boy or girl who lived nearby could attend any of the hobby groups. However, Maxim did not come to be attending the ensemble of his own accord. Once he was at a singing lesson back in March, and his singing was heard by a grave-looking man with tufted, ginger eyebrows (at first everybody had thought that he was an official, inspecting the school). So, he heard it and said to Maxim after the lesson in a deep strict voice:

"Well, my dear fellow, come with me. Immediately."

Maxim went willingly because he wasn't afraid of that severe man at all, and after the singing lesson there was to be a dictation test.

They came to the Palace of Culture and entered a large room where there was a shiny grand piano. Its upper lid resembled a killer whale's slanting fin, and the piano keys, its teeth. The man with the tufted eyebrows began pressing different keys and asked Maxim to repeat the music with his voice. It wasn't difficult at all, and Maxim repeated it, although in a quiet voice because he was shy. Then the man began to play the song about a grasshopper which was eaten by a shameless frog — everybody knows that song. And Maxim had to sing it. Probably he didn't manage it very well. The man stopped playing, stood Maxim between his knees and said not angrily but rather pleadingly:

---

[1] Chkalov — the famous Russian pilot of 1930s. Culture palaces (in the former USSR) were large buildings built by factories where adults and children spent their free time attending different hobby groups. (—Tr.)

"What's the matter, old fellow? Don't be shy please. I am sure that singing is a thing you like doing very much."

Maxim grew a little bolder and said:

"Uh-huh."

"Do you sing at home when alone? I am sure you do."

Maxim grew more bold and answered:

"It depends on the song."

The man was happy:

"That's nice! Great! What kind of songs do you like? Go on!"

Suddenly Maxim remembered that after the dictation test was a natural history lesson, and, by chance, he had forgotten to do his homework assignment. And he asked:

"Do you play the guitar? I can't do it with the piano somehow...."

The teacher darted off his round chair, dashed away and returned in no time with a shiny guitar.

"What will you sing? Tell me!"

"I don't know the name...."

"Well, we'll see. You start it and I'll find the melody."

Maxim started and he was probably not very good:

"Bonfire is barely glowing
And darkness has covered the camp."

The guitar overtook his voice, and it became easier. But it was the kind of song that must be sung properly if you're going to sing it at all, because it seems at once that danger is everywhere around, and very soon everybody will rush to attack.

"No time to unsaddle our horses
And sing some songs at day's end..."

Further on Maxim didn't know himself how he sang. But, apparently, his voice sounded clear and with emotion because the words of that song were themselves alarming and clear:

"In frail scary silence
The darkness and light reverse
The hammers in the rebels' rifles
Cocked like their nerves...."

When the song ended, the teacher put the guitar aside and said thoughtfully:

"Well, well, it's interesting.... Where did you hear this song?"

"From my brother."

"Does he sing too?" quickly asked the teacher.

"Ah, no. It's on his tape recorder."

"Well, okay, Maxim Rybkin. My name is Anatoly Fedorovich, and I am the conductor of the children's chorus. And I ask you, my old fellow, don't run away, please."

Maxim didn't. Why? At least he could sing here and not be shy of it. Not like at home, where Andrew could hear him and start teasing. Although, there were some songs Maxim didn't like. But it couldn't be helped. Nobody likes everything in this world. On the other hand, there was a song, "The First Flight", and for Maxim it was the best.

This was the song he would perform at the local TV studio, in the concert devoted to The Pioneer Day.

Maxim moved his field cap to the left side and with pleasure looked at himself in the mirror once more. It was good. Although his papa and mama weren't pilots and he had never flown himself, even as a passenger, he would sing of pilots, and the little wings on his field cap were just what was needed.

Of course, he would look better still if his ears were a bit smaller and wouldn't protrude so much. And if he had dark and wavy hair as his brother had, but shorter. And his lips could be thinner, and his nose could be more straight and manly, like Papa's. But, well, it couldn't be helped. In general, Maxim was good as he was.

You can say whatever you like, but a man's appearance is a very important thing. Maxim became a soloist just because of it. Of course, nobody told him this, but he had guessed. Once, after a rehearsal, he happened to hear an argument between Anatoly Fedorovich and Aleftina Eduardovna, the ensemble's director.

Anatoly Fedorovich was only outwardly grave; in reality he was a very kind man. He never shouted at the children even if they played about at rehearsals. But on this occasion he spoke with Aleftina Eduardovna very heatedly. They had quarreled because of Alex Tigritsky.

"Have pity on the child!" said Anatoly Fedorovich indignantly. "You enjoy his voice as if it's candy, but all the chorus becomes distracted and starts giggling when Alex is singing, 'Comrade pilot, take me, I am so light!'"

It was true, and they chuckled. Standing in the wings, Maxim again barely stopped laughing. For indeed, when Alex, nicknamed "Chief Cook", went to the microphone, with his fat knees and his round belly looking like a tight sack, the stage boards began creaking.

"But, dear Anatoly Fedorovich," Aleftina Eduardovna argued endearingly, "we have a chorus, not a ballet group. So, we must think about the sound—"

"Art — that's the thing we must think of!" almost snarled Anatoly Fedorovich. "That's all! When in the middle of a serious song we hear laughter in the hall, who needs this damn good sound! And what about poor Tigritsky himself? Oh, no, let him sing about macaroni — it would be a perfect harmony: in appearance, voice and content."

"But what about 'The First Flight' song? This ensemble is named after the great pilot, after all!"

"You shall have it. Alex is not the only one with a good voice here."

The next day, Anatoly Fedorovich stopped Maxim after the rehearsal and asked him warily:

"Maximushka[1].... Will you manage with 'The First Flight'?"

Of course, he knew that Maxim liked that song best of all. Maxim got a bit scared and shy. And he asked in a whisper:

"Don't know.... Should I sing it in the concert too?"

"We'll see. Let's try it."

---

[1] "Ushka" is another Russian addition to the names of children, to make them softer and show somebody's favor. (—Tr.)

The first time it didn't go very well, because Aleftina Eduardovna came up and looked at Anatoly Fedorovich with her lips pursed. Maxim got out of time.

"Well, well," said Anatoly Fedorovich pensively. "Well, Rybkin. We'll try... some more, next time."

Maxim felt sorry for him. He got a bit angry and said:

"Can we try it once again?"

"Again? You want to do this?"

Maxim nodded, closed his eyes tight and imagined the morning sky, the white fluffy clouds and the daisy eyes fluttering under the plane wings.... He imagined it so well that he missed the beginning of the song.

"Oh, sorry. Can we start again?"

And the song started:

> "The sun has just arisen
> A breeze has touched the grass.
> The town's little airfield has awoken all at once."

It was a little airfield with some small sport planes. The pilots were preparing engines. And some boys were standing at the edge of the field — those who wanted to rise to the sky very much. Those who fly in their dreams.

Maxim had such dreams almost every night....

He finished singing and became afraid again. Was it all right?

Anatoly Fedorovich smiled. He looked at Aleftina Eduardovna and said: "Aha?"

Then he looked at Maxim and showed him the thumbs up.

Of course, Alex's voice was better than Maxim's; no doubt about that. He had been singing longer than Maxim. And his second name, Tigritsky[1], was much more dignified for a soloist than Rybkin. But the flight is the flight; even if it's a song and not real. What could be done if Alex weighed fifty kilograms and Maxim half as much!

And, probably, that wasn't the main thing. It seemed to Maxim that it was all the same to Alex what kind of

---

[1] Tigritsky — derived from the word "tiger" (—Tr.)

song to sing. Songs of macaroni and of pilots he sang equally well. Probably Alex didn't fly in his dreams. And not without reason he was indifferent to their new uniform with the little wings on the field cap.

The uniform was so good! Even the children from the older group were envious of it. Of course, not the guys who had a bass voice, but those who had moved there just recently. No wonder! They didn't have such field caps.

And how was it possible to go in the field cap and without the uniform? Mama didn't understand it.

"Maxim, at least put on a jacket."

Andrew glanced back and smiled. Now he would say: "Oh, Ma, stop it! What jacket are you talking about? He must shine everywhere. Just imagine, our artist is going along the streets, and the passers-by are turning around: 'Ah, is it the boy who's just been on TV? Ah, did he sing the main song? Who can imagine it, what a boy!'"

And the most unpleasant thing was that he was right. For Andrew had a nasty peculiarity: he could see through Maxim.

"Oh, Ma, stop it!" Andrew started, and Maxim's soul shrunk. "What jacket are you talking about...? It's a real summer outdoors. Let him toughen himself up."

No, sometimes his brother could be rather good. Mama said that all this would end with her death and ordered Maxim to get out.

"And don't be late for lunch. Can we have it together like all normal people, at least on Saturday?"

"Mam, I can't be on time! The concert will have ended by one o'clock, and I am to be at school at a half past one. No time for lunch."

"Well, well. But why are you going without your satchel?"

"We haven't any lessons today. We're going on an excursion to the park."

"I can imagine how your uniform will look after that.... Don't forget to have dinner in the canteen."

"Yep— Oh, and what about money?"

"What a scatterbrain! Have you forgotten it?"

"No, I haven't. It's just gone."

"Spent? But your pockets are jingling!"

Mama went to the room and brought Maxim's school trousers and jacket. She shook them, and indeed some clinking was heard.

"But it's not money," Maxim said hurriedly. "It's just some things... I didn't have time to take them out."

And he hastily started to extract those clinking things: two nuts tied with a piece of string, a yellow brass key, a camera film spool without the lid, a big old coin and a broken cuff link.

"Other parents have normal children, but I've got a Plushkin," said Mama in a pensive voice. "Put your treasures away immediately."

"I will, I will."

Next to the shoe shelf there was a plasterboard box. Mama called Maxim "Plushkin" because of the things he had stored there.

Plushkin was a greedy landowner from Gogol's novel "Dead Souls." Maxim hadn't read it, but he watched it on TV. It was not very interesting, but Maxim watched it anyway, to see how much Plushkin resembled him.

No, Maxim was not a Plushkin. That man was a crazy miser, but Maxim just felt sorry for discarded things.

Let's take, for instance, a very small thing: a badge with "D" and a football — "Dynamo" football team. Somebody had spent time making it, then it was probably on a football fan's chest. And then — oops! it had found itself on the pavement: its pin had broken off. Poor badge! Who would have felt sorry for it if Maxim had not found it? The pin could be mended, and somebody would be happy to have it.

Or this one: a faceted glass cork from a decanter. Of course, it was hard to find a proper decanter for it, but you could wind a rope on it and make the cork spin. Or, you could look through it. Everything became blurred and dancing, and multicolored sunlight spots flew around like butterflies.

Plushkin gave nothing to anybody, but Maxim was not greedy. If you need something — please, you could take this cork, and the badge, and the small bearing, and the wheels from a toy truck, and the blue cracked ash-tray, and the plastic soldiers, and the coils of wire... the main thing, it must be for the common good: both for the people and things.

"Leave your salvage alone and listen to me," said Mama. "I don't have small coins now. So, take five rubles and make sure not to lose the change."

Maxim got slightly offended: "Did I ever lose it?"

"Well, you didn't. At least this isn't your way. But who knows.... Where are you going to put the money?"

The uniform had only one small breast pocket. Mama pushed the folded five-ruble note and two tram tickets in there.

"Be careful, don't shake it out. And where will you put your handkerchief?"

"Oh, why, I don't need it. Mam, I'll run!"

Mama smiled, took Maxim by his ears, drew him closer and kissed him on his nose.

"Go on, I wish you good luck."

"Have fun!" cried Papa from his room.

"Be cool, bro," said Andrew.

Chapter two

ABOUT FUN, FEAR AND BOLDNESS

Sometimes, some people feel that they have tight, ringing strings in their bodies. Especially when you look through the window and see a clear sunny morning. Or, you know that something nice is about to happen. And you, agile, quick and good-looking, are skipping downstairs from the third floor. The clattering of your sandals flies somewhere behind — tra-ta-ta-ta-ta! In a moment, in half a second, right now, the porch door will rebound from your palms, and the spring streets will rush towards you!

Hurrah!

Oh, no....

It seemed Mama was right. Maybe it was better to return home?

But after such a start there was no going back. In addition, it would be a bad omen: you wouldn't have good luck. And Maxim really needed good luck today!

He hugged his shoulders and shivered. Then he stood for a while in the middle of the yard, breathing into his hands and rubbing his legs, which were covered with goose bumps. But it was nothing. He wasn't a frail old lady muffled in her warm clothes and trembling with cold. Soon he would get used to it. Besides, it would be probably warmer on the sunny side of the street. Come on!

Indeed, it was not very cold in the sun. One-two, one-two! And soon Maxim stopped shivering and marched quickly along the sunny street, avoiding the shades of the poplars, which had recently been cropped in the form of fluffy balls.

The poplars' long green catkins dangled in the wind. In time they would ripen, and their tickling fuzz would fly over the whole town. But it would be later, when the leaves become larger. For the time being they were small and pointed. A kindergarten of small leaves. Even from afar you could see they were sticky and fresh.

The buds' scales were scattered all over the asphalt and looked like small open beaks. They were sticky, too, and stuck to Maximka's[1] new sandals. They stopped clicking because of that, but anyway Maxim tried to go with a firm tread. And it seemed that the passers-by looked with pleasure at such a well-tempered boy in his unusual uniform....

The street was climbing up; the big buildings ended, and farther on began a street with small wooden houses. And there!

Astride on the gate, sat — drat him! — Vitka Transya (his full nickname was "Transistor"). He was fastening something; it seemed to be a weather vane.

But it wasn't important what he was fixing there; the main thing was that he was sitting there, looking around. And it was impossible to pass by him unnoticed.

Maxim slowed his steps, sighed angrily and... turned

---

[1] *Maximka — the addition "ka" is often used in Russia with children names. It adds lightness and informality. (—Tr.)*

to the right.

Of course, it was not very brave conduct. But what else could he do? That mean Transya would certainly block his way. Maybe he would be too lazy to get off the gate if Maxim were in his usual clothes, but after seeing Maximka's new cherry-colored uniform he would certainly come and stand in his way.

"Ah, what a nice little chap goes by! Aren't you smart! What a waistcoat, what shorts, what buttons— Hey, you stop when an older boy talks to you! That's better. Ah, just look at this field cap! Give it to me to try on...."

But what could he do? Argue? It was useless. Run away? The shame of it. Stand and wait? Transya would take his field cap, and nobody knew what would happen next. Maybe he would give it back, and maybe he would throw it on the roof. After that he might trip Maxim up and drag him in the dirt. Then, after picking him up, he would brush him down for fun and say mockingly, "Oh, poor little boy, what a misfortune...."

Oh, Transya, the big bully.... What happiness it would be if he fell off that gate! He always picked on those who were weaker, and Maxim had very often got in trouble. Transya could steal up from behind, stop his mouth with one hand and then pull his hair. Then he would give it him in the neck and shove him away. And it happened everywhere: in the streets, in school.

Maxim imagined Transya's smile — thin and long. His eyes, despite his smiling, were somewhat dull. On his lip he had a pimple, and his face looked as if it was covered with gray dust. Perhaps it was from smoking. Transya smoked every day with senior pupils in a school toilet. Everybody knew it, but it was useless to scold him. So, what could be done with him when he barred the way? What indeed? To be honest, Maxim knew what. Transya was not much stronger, and he was only a bit taller than Maxim.... Courage could help here, but Maxim was a coward.

Perhaps, though nobody knew it. But Maxim knew within himself that he was a coward. You can't deceive yourself. Sometimes you forget it, but then you are afraid of something else, and your soul is heavy again. And nothing can be done. You have to live anyway. Cowards are people too. And their lives are uneasy: cowards must do everything normal people do, and take care that nobody knows about their timidity.

There was a hope, however, that cowardice would end by itself. They say that people's characters change with age. Maybe Maxim's character would change too. Maybe it would even happen soon. And then Transya wouldn't be so glad. Even today, Maxim was not very much afraid of him. He probably wouldn't have turned into the side street if he had not been wearing his new uniform.

After all, he shouldn't let Vitka Transistor get on his nerves before such an important performance. He just had no right. He had to be in a cheerful mood.... And the day itself was too great to spoil it. The sky reflected in the windowpanes as in dark water, and the sunbeams bounced back in hot flashes. He had to go on!

Well, now, it seemed, he was to turn to the left and come out onto Titov Street[1] with the tramlines.

Maxim turned and found himself in a side street where he had never been before. No wonder, Maxim's parents had moved to this town recently, just after the winter holidays.

The town where Maxim had lived before had been built near a large factory plant. The houses in that town were high, similar looking blocks of flats. The streets were straight, without intricate bends and alleyways. At the time, Maxim thought that all towns must be like that. But when he came here he saw a fine assortment of constructions. Twelve-storied buildings rose above the wooden houses and old buildings of red brick with wrought iron balconies. The street named after Gogol passed by a new food store and suddenly ended near a tall church with turrets, cupolas and narrow windows. The church looked very interesting, although nobody had prayed there for a long time, and the town's movie distribution firm was located in its premises.

Sometimes it seemed to Maxim that his new town was filled with all kinds of secrets and hidden treasures.

---

[1] *Gherman Titov, the second Soviet cosmonaut. (—Tr.)*

Indeed, once a local paper told that when some builders had been demolishing an old house they had found a tin of gold coins, inside one of the walls. They had been hidden by some merchant long ago. But the coins were rubbish. Probably, you could even find real weapons because long ago this town had seen many battles during the Civil War.[1]

Certainly, the old garrets could hide all kinds of things. It would be great to find a Mauser or a cavalry sword! You could hand it over to the museum, and they would display it in the most prominent place. But first of all, it would be great to play with it. Then Vitka Transya would be as quiet as a mouse.

What a pity Maxim now lived in a new five-storied block of flats, and not in that little old house where some carpenters were repairing the gate.

The gate was big and attractive. Its darkened door flaps were covered with a wooden pattern resembling the sun. The gate leaned to one side and, probably for that reason, the owner had decided to replace the gateposts.

Two men were wielding their axes, hewing out a crossbeam from a pine log.

Maxim stopped. The fresh-cut wood shone so brilliantly! It looked as if it was made of gold. And the chips which flew in all directions were gold too. One chip — long and wide — landed on the grass near Maxim.

Maxim fearlessly stepped closer. The carpenters weren't like Vitka Transya; they wouldn't bully him.

"Excuse me," said Maxim in a high-pitched voice, "can I take this chip?"

The carpenters straightened up. The first man was young and glum. Without leaving hold of his axe, he took out a pack of cigarettes and put one in his mouth, having flicked it out with his finger. Then he began to grope for matches. The other man put his axe aside and looked at Maxim. He was old, with silver stubble on his thin chin and hollow cheeks. His eyes were bright blue.

"Who's chirping here?" said the old man and smiled as though he was very glad to see Maxim. His few teeth were

---

[1] *The Civil War in Russia was in 1917-1922. (—Tr.)*

smoke-stained. "A chip for you? Ah, well, take it. Take them all if you like. What are you going to do with it? It's for kindling, is it?"

"No, it's like a sword" explained Maxim and waved his hand.

"Well, fighter, take it, take your sword!"

"Thank you!"

And Maxim walked away, looking back occasionally at the kind old man. The carpenters began hewing the log again, but the old man held onto his axe for a moment and looked after Maxim.

The chip was wonderful. One side of it was covered with the copper colored scales of bark; the other, freshly cut side had a strong pine aroma. Maxim walked along, tapping his knees with this side, and small resin drops stuck to his skin.

The narrow sidewalk led him along a low fence made of unpainted slats. Next to it some quite big burdocks had already grown. Among them were last year's dusty stalks. There was one old burdock even taller than Maximka.

Maxim showed respect for live plants, but this one was dried up; it was a perfect target to try out his sword. Maxim swung his hand and chopped. Thwack! But the thick stalks turned out as hard as a wire. The burdock tops were quivering, but didn't fall. Crack! Zap! The sharp edge of the chip had already become blunt, but the stubborn burdock stood as if mocking him—

"Hey, what are you doing, you hooligan? Get out of here!"

A woman's head appeared over the fence. She was probably the owner of the garden. Maxim saw the turban of hair tied up with a pink scarf, small earrings and very angry eyes. He was startled at first, and then said with wonder:

"I am not a hooligan! I am just playing!"

"'Just playing!' Brandishing your stick like a windmill!"

"But why, it's just an old burdock."

"Go home and chop what you like there!"

"What a silly grumbler," thought Maxim, but politely said aloud:

"This burdock is not yours. It's growing in the street."

The woman in the pink scarf moved her lips, took a deep breath, and then burst out:

"Oh, just look at him!... 'is not yours!' A good boy to look at, but speaks to adults so cheekily! Just you wait, I'll let my dog loose!"

Maxim was not afraid of the dog. But there was no use arguing, so he went on his way. He didn't even feel upset; he just thought that people are so different....

The chip had become damaged and was no longer fit to be a weapon. But Maxim felt sorry for it — it had just served him as a sword.

Titov Street, with its flitting red and yellow trams, could already be seen at the end of the side street. Near it Maxim noticed a blue pool; probably it remained after the night's rain. That was nice! Let the chip be a little ship. At the edge of the sidewalk Maxim picked up an empty matchbox. The chip became a ship's hull, and the box, a cabin. Have a good trip!

Cleaving through the water, the steamer was going to the other shore. But Maxim didn't run after it. He squatted down over the pool and looked at the reflected sky. There, very deep below, in the dark-blue air, flew a light woolly cloud. And at the edge of the sky Maxim saw himself — neat and good-looking as before, with the white triangle of his shirt in the cut of his waistcoat, the little wings on his field cap and a red star badge above his breast pocket.

Soon, Maxim would no longer wear this badge. The day after tomorrow he would become a Pioneer[1]. Many children in his class became Pioneers in the winter, but Maxim did not. At that time, the Chief Pioneer Leader Rimma Vasilievna had told him:

"Rybkin, you are a new person here. First prove that

---

[1] *The Pioneer Organization — a school organization in the former USSR. It was like the scout organization for the children of 8-12 years old. The Pioneers wore red neck-ties. Younger pupils were usually called "Oktyabryata" or "Children of October," and they wore little red stars badges with the portrait of Lenin, when he was a young boy. Lenin led the Revolution in 1917. Children were convinced that it was a great honor when you become a Pioneer (—Tr.)*

you are ready to be admitted, and in May we'll decide."

Maxim had been upset then: he didn't know how he could prove it. But, apparently, he had done something good because they decided to admit him at the next Pioneer meeting. Probably they wouldn't change their decision, especially if they saw him singing on television....

Maxim's thoughts were interrupted by a siren. An ambulance turned into the side street at full speed. Life is a very complicated thing: one person can have a festive day, while another has misfortune. Maxim jumped off the pool so that the car would not splash him and he followed it with his eyes. Next to the driver sat a woman in a white doctor's coat and a white cap. Svetlana Sergeevna, a school nurse who had once given vaccinations to Maxim's class, had a cap like this.

When Maxim thought of Svetlana Sergeevna anxiety started gnawing at him. That day, pupils had been called, one after another, to the school aid post. For Maxim that eerie moment had happened during a reading lesson. And when Sofia Iosifna, the class teacher, had told him to go there Maxim couldn't cope with his fear. He had stood up and informed her in a very serious voice:

"But I've recently had an injection at my old school. It could harm me if I have it again."

"Really?" said the class teacher suspiciously; "then, it must be recorded on your medical card."

"I don't know. But I certainly had an injection. I didn't even go to school the next day because of a high temperature, and it hurt a little."

Maxim had been lying with the cold despair of a man in mortal danger. Fear was the strongest thing he had inside.

Maxim had been vaccinated just twice — in the first and the second grade. But his fear had been constant, because who knew when the next time would be? Of course, Maxim didn't think of his fear always, but when going to school he thought it could happen any time. And if he saw a doctor's coat in the school corridor he began to worry at once: were they preparing? When he heard the clattering of women's heels during a lesson, he shuddered and imagined that it was a nurse or a doctor. Probably the doctor was going along the corridor, with a round, shiny box of syringes in her hand. They look like huge mosquitoes with transparent bellies and merciless stings. When the syringe plunger is being pressed you see a very thin jet, and then a small drop hangs at the end of the needle. And then... "Come on, boy, turn around, don't be afraid...." It's easy to say, "Don't be afraid!"

And you feel terrible, not only because of the pain. Much worse is the expectation, quiet metal clinking and a sinking heart. And the inevitability. There is nowhere to run away or hide. You have to force yourself to smile and pretend that all this is a mere trifle, because there is one thing that is more awful than an injection. Mockery! If somebody knew that you were a coward....

Last time, cunning and looking like a prickly sea horse Mishka Stremenenko had already looked at Maxim suspiciously....

So Maxim could not bear it. He had deceived the teacher, although he understood that his trickery could soon be exposed.

But it wasn't. Probably they believed him. Or they forgot about Maxim in the bustle of the school day. But his fear had not gone: what if they learned that he had deceived them? It would be awful. First, he would inevitably get an injection. Second, all the class would laugh at him. And Rimma Vasilievna would say: "And you, Rybkin, hope to become a Pioneer after telling such a lie?"

However, today there was an excursion, and Maxim would be in school only for a short time. Tomorrow would be Sunday, and on Monday was the Pioneer meeting where he would become a Pioneer. Surely nothing would come to light until then. And further on, the holidays were at hand.

Maxim thought that probably he would grow up and become stronger. He would train his will power and courage. Even now he felt that he had become a bit bolder lately. Some time ago he had been afraid of singing before the public, but now he wasn't. Well to tell the truth, he was, but only a tiny little bit. He was a bit nervous.

Well, he had to get going; the time till the concert was

running out quickly.

It's time! Maxim just wanted to take a step and— Oh! next to his sandal he saw a wonderful thing! It was a bolt with a hexagon head and a nut screwed on it. It was as long as Maxim's little finger and a bit thicker than a pencil. A beautiful new *boltik* with a fresh, sharp thread. This kind of thing comes in useful for everything!

The boltik was trodden into the damp soil. Maxim picked it out, hurriedly washed it in the pool and wiped it with a plantain leaf.

What a pity, he had nothing to put the boltik into. It would be conspicuous in his flat breast pocket and, besides, it was not very clean. Very well, he could carry it in his hand! A good find was a good omen. It meant that everything would be all right.

Chapter three

THE FLIGHT

The television studio was located in the district where Maxim had not yet been. But it was difficult to get lost — the TV tower was almost two hundred meters high and was visible from all around. You could get to it on foot or by tram. Anatoly Fedorovich explained to Maxim that it was the third stop for the TV center.

The tram had some free seats, but Maxim did not sit down. He went to the rear platform and leaned there with his back against the window, stretching his hands over the handrail. The sun started burning his shoulders through the glass; the street was running behind the window flitting away with brightly colored signboards, big trees and shop windows.

Maxim had looked at the street for some time, and then he began to examine his boltik. Its hexahedral head had the engraved number "12". The nut went smoothly along the threading, not very loosely and not too tight. It was not a screw, but a wonder! Even Mama would probably not say that Maxim was a Plushkin, because such a boltik should be liked by anyone.

At the third stop Maxim leapt out onto the sunny asphalt and at once craned his neck. The latticed TV tower soared to an awesome height right above him. Its aerials were barely visible among the scanty white clouds and they looked like arrow flights. If only he could climb up there!

But there was no chance. The tower was behind a high, mesh fence; in that fence there was a checkpoint: a small, attractive house with two windows and a door. Next to the door stood a stout woman wearing a beret with a star, a blue coat and a big holster. The holster hung on two straps — military sailors and pilots wear their holsters like this. Maxim noticed at once that under the leather flap there was a gun with a ring at the back of its handle. That meant it was a revolver.

Maxim looked around. Where were the other children? They had been told clearly to gather next to the entrance. Maxim tentatively approached the woman with the gun.

"Excuse me, please. Our chorus is going to sing at the concert, and we are to meet here. Have you seen the other children here?"

The women turned around and smiled broadly:

"Aha, one more artist! What a smart uniform you've got. Yes, I know that you are to come. But the other children are inside already. I was told to let you in straightaway. It's cold today, but many have come inadequately dressed, like you. Aren't you cold?"

Well, really! Maxim had quite forgotten the chill of the morning. Now in the street it was a real summer's day. Even the light breeze did not make him feel cold.

"Come in, come in, little finch," said the woman, moving aside a little. Maxim slipped into the gap between her round side and the doorpost. And stopped. Next to him, unbelievably close, he saw again the holster with the handle sticking out.

"It's loaded, is it?" asked Maxim deferentially, and gave the woman a serious look. (If only he could touch it, at least with his finger! But, of course he wouldn't be allowed to.)

"Yes, it is," said the woman with a sigh. "What's the use of carrying it if it's not loaded?"

"And the cartridges are blank or live?"

The guard woman smiled again.

"Blank cartridges are used only when they shoot movies. And I am on sentry duty."

"Do you catch saboteurs?" guessed Maxim. "If they creep inside and blow this tower up so much iron will fall on the houses around!"

"Nobody will get in while I am here," the woman consoled him and stroked her holster. "Even a cockroach won't creep by me, let alone a saboteur. But good people are always welcome.... Well, run to the studio and get warm — look, your knees are almost blue from cold."

"No, they aren't blue," said Maxim condescendingly. "It's some resin stuck from a pine chip."

And he hopped across the yard on one leg; the other he raised to rub off the resin dots with spit on his finger. But then he gave up. Anyway, it wasn't possible to remove it all at once. And, also, resin is not dirt. They say some people cure rheumatism with it....

The studio vestibule had already filled with people. Here were the girls from the dancing group; guys from the senior groups, long-haired like Andrew; the children from the orchestra with their big instrument-cases and, of course, the fellows from "The Little Wings."

Mama was right: most children had come in coats, jackets or tracksuits. But Maxim was also partly right: some boys were dressed like him — they weren't afraid of the cold. And it wasn't only the people from "The Little Wings." Near the door Maxim saw a round faced, gray-eyed boy in the same uniform, but his field cap was bluish-green. It meant he was a musician.

Maxim wondered: the boy wasn't older than him but he played in the orchestra! It was interesting, which instrument would he play? Maybe Maxim should ask him? No, it was somehow inconvenient.

Maxim wanted to run to the children of his chorus, but he saw that the boy-musician was looking at him with a twinkling eye. Then he came over to Maxim, put his head on one side and asked:

"What's your name?"

Maxim liked the way he looked, and that the boy came up without any shyness. And he quickly answered:

"I'm Maxim."

"Maxim, buy an elephant off me!"

"Which... elephant?"

The boy's eyes became mischievous and he said:

"Everybody says 'Which elephant?' Don't ask, just buy it."

Maxim guessed that it was a kind of game. But he did not show that he guessed because he took a liking to the boy, and the game was funny.

"I would buy it," he said.

The boy answered at once:

"Everybody says 'I would buy it!' Go on and buy."

It was the game where the seller and the buyer had to invent what to reply. If one of them failed, he was the loser. At first it was funny, but then Maxim imagined that he saw that elephant. It was tied by its leg to a thick post. And at once he felt sorry for it. The elephant stood big and sad, and nobody wanted to buy it, but only invented excuses.

"If I had money, I would," said Maxim seriously.

"Everybody says 'If I had money!' Get some money and buy."

"I wonder, is my room big enough for it?"

The boy smiled.

"Everybody asks 'Is my room enough?'! So, will you buy it?"

"OK, I will"

"Everybody says 'I will!' But have you got—" And at that moment they were caught by Margarita Penkina the chorus leader, a big girl.

"Rybkin! Where are you wandering about? Anatoly Fedorovich is already gathering everyone together! It's time to warm up!"

"Oh, oh, oh!" said Maxim mockingly, so the orchestra boy would not think that he was afraid of Margo. "Where am I wandering? Maybe I am one hundred miles away?"

He said goodbye to the boy with his eyes and went

after Penkina. They were going up a lengthy corridor and Maxim looked at the back of Margo's head, where her big white bows with black dots were bobbing up and down.

"Penkina, buy an elephant," he said.

"Leave me alone!" she snapped without turning around. "What on earth! All the boys have gone crazy with this elephant. I am beside myself with worry because of the concert, and you're playing stupid games...."

Ha, ha, "beside myself with worry." Maybe Maxim was nervous too, but he didn't shout about it over the whole corridor.

They came to the room where "The Little Wings" had already gathered together. All the walls of that room were covered with mirrors, and it seemed, because of that, the room was filled with a whole one thousand people. They were thronging, talking, laughing, and exclaiming from accidental and non-accidental elbow shoves. Those who had come in coats laid them on the long tables. What a muddle there would be afterwards!

Alex Tigritsky pulled off his huge shaggy sweater and cheerfully turned to Maxim. He was not angry at all that Maxim was going to sing the song about the flight instead of him.

"Hey, Rybkin, buy an elephant!"

"I know this stuff," said Maxim.

"Everybody says 'I know this stuff—'" gladly began Alex. But at that moment they heard the voice of Anatoly Fedorovich:

"Folks! A minute of your attention! We're beginning soon. So for a while, let's run through everything...."

And then Maxim understood what Margo meant, saying that she was beside herself with worry.

After the concert hall in the palace, the studio looked rather small. Instead of a stage there were some steps and platforms of different heights. The auditorium was without chairs, and the audience was sitting on the steps in a semicircle, similar to a stadium. Children from different schools were already seated there in their Pioneer uniforms. The girls and boys from the ensemble also sat among them, waiting for their turn. Then, the numerous floodlights under the ceiling had been turned on. And the huge floodlights on the high tripods, too. They were covered with white gauze, or else you would be dazzled completely.

On the floor, the cameramen were rolling their heavy cameras on the high stands, and numerous cables twisted behind them. Anatoly Fedorovich appeared again.

"Hey, 'The Little Wings!' Fly to the stage, quickly!"

What? It was time? Maxim felt even slightly sick with anxiety. But for a while it was only a rehearsal, or, to be more exact, the TV men wanted to decide where the children would stand or sit on the stage. It turned out, that the chorus would not stand in three ranks as usual, but they would sit randomly on the stage steps and on the big plywood cubes.

"The children will be more natural like this," said a curly haired girl with a microphone on her chest.

Anatoly Fedorovich knitted his thick brows.

"It's very unusual for them. Couldn't you have told us beforehand?"

"Oh, well, I am sure you'll be fine! Will you manage it, children?"

"The Little Wings" yelled gaily that they would. It was more interesting to sit down than standing in rows.

"It wouldn't be a bad idea to rehearse," said Anatoly Fedorovich. But the girl with the microphone explained hurriedly that they had no time for a rehearsal: "The lighting technicians dragged out their work, and we are pressed for time."

Anatoly Fedorovich looked after her and called Alex and Maxim.

"Well, how are you, colleagues? Nervous?"

Alex shook his head. He had had lots of experience and never had butterflies in his stomach. But Maxim sighed and said:

"A little bit...."

"Never mind, never mind. Do it well, please. The things are not going as we thought— Hey, Maximushka, what's up with your hand?"

Nothing was up with his hand; it was something in his hand. The boltik. Maxim had still been carrying it in his fist. He undid his fingers and showed his find:

"There's nowhere to put it," he complained.

His palm was sweating, red with the remains of grease and the threading imprint.

Anatoly Fedorovich shook his head, took a handkerchief out of his pocket and started to wipe Maxim's palm. Then he wiped the boltik too.

"What's this? Did you arm yourself with a talisman, so as not to be afraid, eh?"

"No, I've just found it. But my pocket's small."

"Ah! I thought it was an amulet for you, for courage. Are you going to sing with it?"

"Can I?"

"Well... you can, I think. But please, try your best."

Maxim nodded... and felt that his nervousness had ended. He felt somehow relaxed, comfortable and even a bit sleepy. It was probably because of the warmth. The numerous lamps and floodlights warmed the air so much that it became as hot as an African beach. Maxim looked sympathetically at the older boys: they were roasting in their suits....

"The Little Wings" had scattered again in the auditorium; the other groups, in turn, were going to the stage in front of the cameras, and TV men were trying them on and arguing.

At last a voice, from somewhere above, said: "Everybody attention! Now we are beginning!"

The senior chorus, in blue jackets and bell-bottomed trousers, started forming their ranks on the stage.

A young woman, in a fluffy red pullover, came out in front of them. She smiled and started speaking distinctly and with animation:

"Dear children! Dear television viewers! Today, you'll see a gala performance by young performers of our town. Of course, our young singers, musicians and dancers are not real performers for a while. They are children like you. But they very much like to sing, dance and play musical instruments. They've learned all these things in their Pioneer ensemble."

Then there appeared a fifth grader, Svetka Danilevskaya. In the complete silence her voice was very clear and resonant:

"Now, we invite on the stage the Chkalov Culture Palace's Children's Musical Choreographic Ensemble!"

Then, for about five minutes, she said who the art director was, the concertmaster, the composer.... At last, the senior group started singing.

Maxim knew the entire program by heart, and he was almost not listening to them. He watched the cameramen mostly, because sometimes the cameras turned to the audience. It meant that all the people could see Maxim on television! And Mama could, and Papa, and Andrew. And his classmates, too....

Maxim did his best trying to sit in a dignified way, squeezing the boltik in his fist.

The chorus had sung two songs about cosmonauts and one more, about competition between the Pioneers. After that the orchestra came on the stage. To be more exact, not the whole orchestra, but several younger children. They were carrying big tubas, flutes and a drum. And the silver colored contrabass was of such a big size that its little owner was completely hidden behind it; you could see only his legs and a blue field cap. The drum was also a giant. However, the girl-drummer was not small and thin, but quite tall and sturdy.

And in front of the orchestra stood the boy that Maxim had met in the vestibule, and who asked him to buy an elephant. He held the brass cymbals. The boy's face was serious. But it seemed to Maxim that behind this seriousness there was hidden a mischievous smile: "Don't think that I am so serious — now I can clash behind the bandmaster so loudly that he will jump up...." Maxim laughed softly and tried to meet his eyes. But the boy stood like a soldier in the ranks, with his heels joined together, hands lowered down and looking straight ahead. Well, anyway Maxim was glad to see him on the stage. He was a good person, and it was a pity that they hadn't met before. But it wasn't to be, because the chorus and orchestra rehearsed on different days....

"Now you'll hear a piece of music from the past!" announced Svetka. "The junior group of the orchestra will perform a march-past of the Kuban marines battalion, 'The King of the Sea'! The conductor is Eugeny Sergeevich Kochkin!"

Eugeny Sergeevich, however, could be called simply Jenya[1]: he appeared just a little older than Maxim's brother Andrew. Eugeny Sergeevich jumped easily onto the stage and raised his hands. The young musician with cymbals looked at the conductor with a little smile. They started playing.

The march was good. Sometimes it sounded sad, but nevertheless it was very energetic. Maxim liked it very much, and best of all he liked the way the boy clashed his cymbals. After clashing he raised his hands on each side and lowered them smoothly down. For some reason he was without his field cap, and after every clash the gust of air made his fair forelock stand on end.

Maxim wished the march would not end. But it couldn't be helped, and it was over. The audience applauded, and Maxim clapped his hands, too, as hard as he could. It was a pity that the boy didn't look at him: probably he didn't notice him among so many boys and girls.

The children from the dance group performed the "Troika" dance, and the turn of "The Little Wings" had come. The little folk in cherry-colored field caps ran to the stage and took the seats they had been assigned at the rehearsal. It couldn't be done, however, without quite a noisy fuss. "Oh, are they showing all this muddle on TV?" thought Maxim anxiously. At last everybody had taken their place.

The three big TV cameras were looking at them with their dark convex lenses. The red lamp on one of them meant that this camera had been turned on. Maxim tried not to look at it. His heart was fluttering, and he had butterflies in his stomach again. But he realized that the song about the flight would be later, and he had some time to take courage.

---

[1] "J" in Jenya has the same sound as the letter "S" in treasure. (—Tr.)

Anatoly Fedorovich stood next to the camera trying not to get into its view. Svetka Danilevskaya again tramped down to the microphone.

"Now, on the stage, the chorus the 'The Little Wings!' The conductor and art director is Anatoly Fedorovich Vershkov."

The audience applauded and the chorus looked at Anatoly Fedorovich. He nodded slightly and raised his hand: attention!

First, the entire chorus sang "The Grasshopper", and how it was gobbled up by a frog. Then Alex sang his "Macaroni." It was a comic song about an Italian who wanted to grow thin, but could not manage it: best of all in this world he liked delicious macaroni. He only had to look at it, and he pounced on it at once.

Alex sang very well and it was funny. The audience laughed and applauded him for a long time. Maxim understood that his moment had come, and his legs went weak.

"I say you, stop it," he said to himself in Mama's strict voice. "Stop it immediately! You must keep yourself in hand!"

It helped a little. Then he saw Anatoly Fedorovich smile at him, and this smile helped too. Indeed, why be nervous? He sang well at the rehearsals, and there was no big difference here. The studio hall was even smaller than in the palace; so was the audience. It was like singing in a room. And he must not think of the TV cameras. That's all....

"The song 'The First Flight!' The soloist is Maxim Rybkin!"

Oh gosh, how quiet it became! Why? Or did it only seem like it to him? Well, he had to go....

Maxim stood up, squeezed the boltik in his fist and bravely went to the microphone. To tell the truth, on his way he had stumbled against the plywood cube where Penkina was sitting, and had nearly lost his balance. But he hadn't. That was OK; probably nobody noticed how he stumbled.

The microphone was like a black rubber pear. This pear stood on the shining stick exactly at the level of

Maximka's chin. Maxim didn't step up too close to it: no need to hide behind it. Anatoly Fedorovich nodded to him: "That's right."

Maxim straightened up and lowered his hands. He would not keep his hands behind him, as Alex did. He would sing not of macaroni, but about pilots.... Then Maxim worried, was his field cap sitting straight? No way to check it now.... Hopefully he wouldn't forget anything.... The main thing was, when the chorus started singing, to imagine at once the airfield and the planes. Of course he would, how could he do anything else? He would at once imagine everything. The sky, the clouds, the grass and the light multicolored planes. And himself, not far from the plane with silvery wings.

The grand piano started. And a moment later the song had begun. But for a while it was not his, Maximka's words. For now the chorus was singing:

> "The sun has just arisen
> A breeze has touched the grass.
> The town's little airfield has awoken all at once.
> The engines rumble merrily
> And flutter daisy eyes.
> The plane is trembling eagerly
> And ready for a flight.
>
> While signals aren't hoisted yet
> By the strict dispatcher man,
> While a pilot hid himself
> In the shadow of his plane,
> The watchman didn't notice
> A boy who'd come inside.
> In grass the boy is standing calmly
> And asking with his eyes..."

To be more convincing Maxim held the boltik harder. He looked over spectators' heads. The searchlights shone and warmed him like the sun in summer. Maxim squinted a little and started singing:

"Comrade pilot!
For you, it's so easy!
I've been waiting a whole three weeks...
For me it's a very important matter,
I want to be a pilot too,
Would you let me fly in your plane right now
Do a miracle, take me with you!"

He was singing, and it already seemed to him that he was indeed asking the pilot to take him on the flight. And if he asked for it very earnestly, with all his strength, then maybe a miracle would indeed happen.

"I don't ask for a taiga or pole
Or for a country that's far away!
I want for a minute to fly over fields
I often dream of it in the night
Take me, I'm very light!"

And then as the last and desperate argument:

"I am not afraid of heights at all
I've jumped twice from the roof!"

And silence. Silence for a second. And every time Maxim stopped at these words he was a little afraid: would the pilot take the boy? He knew that he would, but anyway he earnestly waited while the chorus would dispersed his anxiety. And the chorus finished the song:

"The air was torn by the propeller in shreds
The shrubs and the grass laid down:
The plane with the boy rushed on and took off!
Higher!
   Higher...
      Higher...."

Gradually and smoothly the song had stopped, like the sound of the engine fading when a plane is going down towards the horizon.

And the silence started growing. It became strikingly thick and very long. What was that? What happens next? What should he do now?

And suddenly somebody clapped his hands. And somebody else, then more! And at once, the stormy river of applause overwhelmed Maxim with such a strength that he became afraid of it, even more than of the silence. Oh my, where could all this noise have come from? There weren't that many people here! They were clapping and clapping. Someone even cried "Bravo!", as though it was a real concert with adult singers. Maxim looked back in bewilderment at the chorus. The children were standing and clapping too. Anatoly Fedorovich went up onto the stage, stood next to Maxim and put his hand on Maxim's shoulder. Maxim looked at him in surprise not knowing what to do. Anatoly Fedorovich gave him a smile, then looked at the audience and bowed. The pretty girl in the fluffy red pullover, who had opened the concert, came up and bent over Maxim.

"Your name is Maxim, isn't? My congratulations, Maxim; you sang very well." She straightened up and asked the audience: "Didn't he, girls and boys?"

Again the applause surged like a noisy wind. When it calmed down, she asked:

"Do you like singing songs?"

"Uhh...," he said, embarrassed, in a husky voice. And he checked himself: "Yes, I like it."

"It's your first appearance on stage, isn't?"

"Yes, it is.... That is, it's my first time as a soloist. And on television, too...."

"Well, in that case I have even more reason to congratulate you. It's a very good beginning.... What are you going to be, Maxim?"

Maxim helplessly looked at Anatoly Fedorovich, but he nodded encouragingly: "Keep going!"

"I don't know," said Maxim, almost in a whisper.

"But, nevertheless! Maybe you are going to be a pilot?"

"Maybe," agreed Maxim. But he was not in the mood to pretend, so he repeated: "I don't know.... Really. I haven't decided yet...."

It seemed his answer was not proper. But what could

he say? Maxim frowned and with annoyance rubbed his forehead with his fist. The people in the auditorium began laughing. Maxim quickly lowered his hands. The girl in the fluffy pullover was laughing too.

"It's all right, Maxim. You've got plenty of time to decide.... And what is in your hand?"

"It's... only one thing, a boltik," explained Maxim with embarrassment and opened his little palm.

"How interesting. But why have you brought it?"

It was too long a story to tell it all. Maxim gathered his courage, smiled and said:

"It's for firmness...."

Chapter four

I AM NOT AFRAID OF HEIGHTS AT ALL

At the beginning, summertime looks like a fairy-tale. Then, you get accustomed to it, but the first days are always joyful and festive. And the first day of summer is just a real miracle. Everything is wonderful that day: the smell of a short shower which washed the asphalt (although there was no rain, only a water cart had gone by); the pretty yellow butterflies flitting over lawns; the warm air embracing you from all sides; the hot rays of the sun warming your shoulders through your thin waistcoat and shirt. And there is a beautiful lightness: you are wearing neither a coat nor a tight jacket with an itching collar. You skip about as if bathing in this sunny air. And if you run fast and kick your soles against the asphalt, you can give a great leap and fly to the clouds that hover like big white parachutes.

It's warm, very warm, it's warm everywhere. It's even difficult to believe that this morning the prickly cold scratched your legs and neck. Those who had come to the studio with their warm clothes on now carried their coats on their arms. Only Alex Tigritsky had pulled his sweater on — he guarded his throat from the slightest breeze.

After passing the checkpoint, "The Little Wings" flew away in all directions — to their streets, homes and schools.

Margarita Penkina, the chorus leader, overtook Maxim and said importantly:

"Rybkin, you can become the pride of our ensemble if you work at self-improvement and don't put on airs."

Maxim sighed with annoyance and skipped ahead trying to keep his good mood. Crazy Margaritka! Had he put on airs even once? He was just happy that everything had ended so well. And all the children were glad too: it was a shared song after all.

Maxim's shoulder was still aching — it was Vovka Semenov, who came up and said: "Good for you!" and slapped his shoulder with his palm. It was a friendly slap, of course, but quite hard.

And on his cheek still, there was probably a small red circle with four knobs — an imprint from a button. It was when Anatoly Fedorovich hugged Maxim into his jacket and said, from his heart,

"Good for you, Maximushka, thank you."

But what was there to thank him for? It was he who ought to thank everybody else for what had happened today. Thanks to Anatoly Fedorovich, who taught him and wasn't angry when Maxim confused his notes (to be honest, he confused them even now; yet, they said, he had a good ear that helped him). Thanks to the boy with cymbals and to Alex, that he didn't take offence at him; to Vovka, for his friendly slap; to the girl, the TV presenter, for her good words; to all who listened and clapped; thanks to this summer day, for its warmth and joy; and to the tailor who had made such a fine cherry-colored uniform that was so good for singing and hopping in the sun, when the passers-by look at you, so good-looking, and smile.... And thanks to the hard iron boltik, too.

Maxim was walking on in high spirits, juggling the boltik. But suddenly he realized that it was too early to go to the school.

Where should he go? If he hurried up he could get home and learn what they thought there about the concert. But it would be a rushed, boring conversation.

First, Mama would make him have dinner, but he was not hungry at all. Second, she would tell him to change his clothes because it was the ensemble's uniform. But in his school trousers and jacket he would be cooked alive — the sun simply was doing its best! And he could not put on his new Pioneer uniform either — it had been prepared for the day after tomorrow's Pioneer meeting.

Although, to tell the truth, that wasn't the only thing. Maxim just wanted to look like he had been at the performance. No, it wasn't boasting at all. Well, maybe it was just a little bit.... He simply felt that if he took off "The Little Wings" uniform he would lose some part of his joy. But why?

No, it would be better to go to school right now and spend some time strolling through the neighboring streets he had never been in before. It was a prime time for it, for the streets were literally filled with summer. And almost every street was unknown. He had to explore them all, because now the town was his, Maximka's.

Maxim estimated the direction of his school and turned into a side street.

This street was called Vostochanya[1] Street. It was quiet; its houses were both stone and wooden. Some of them were one-storied, yet more often, two or three-storied. But all of them were old. And the pavement was old too; it was covered not with asphalt but with worn granite slabs. The bright grass and yellow dandelions had already pushed through the cracks; Maxim was walking along trying not to step on them. In one place the slabs had been wrenched out, and the street was crossed by a deep trench. Probably the plumbers were going to replace some old pipes here, but now it was Saturday, and work had stopped. A shaky footbridge was thrown over the trench, but it was some distance away, on the other side of the street. There, near the patterned gate of cast iron, stood two girls, fifth-graders seemingly, who looked at Maxim. Probably they thought that Maxim wouldn't dare jump over the trench and would go to the footbridge.

Maxim looked over the trench and felt tingles down

---

[1] or Eastern Street

his spine. But what should he do? After all, he mustn't chicken out all his life!

"I am not afraid of heights at all
I've jumped twice from the roof!"

He made a step back and squeezed the boltik tight. And then he ran so fast that the wind rushed through his legs. Yay! And he had flown over it! The dark depths of the trench gleamed for a moment with a blue sliver of water, and he fell down on all fours on a pile of mellow clay.

He quickly sprang to his feet, shook off the grains of clay and, not looking at the girls, continued with a confident and independent stride.

But it didn't last long, because all of a sudden he heard a loud, tearful voice. Somebody shouted and wailed behind the corner of a tall house.

Maxim hurriedly went around the corner. There, standing on the pavement he saw a woman in a blue dress and checkered shawl. She was thin like a stick; her shawl covered her hair, forehead and neck. Her head resembled a checkered ball with a small pointed nose. The woman stood upright, like someone on the stage, and was loudly wailing as she looked ahead.

"Oh, we'll burn down! Oh, kind people! The iron! The damned parasite walked out! Oh, if only a car would run over that cursed gallows-bird! Again he'll come back sozzled!"

A fat man in a striped shirt, two women with big bags and another man, very tall and in spectacles, were standing nearby, looking at each other. They couldn't understand why a car should run the iron over, and how it could get sozzled.

Maxim was interested too, and besides, he felt a little sorry for that loudmouthed woman.

Then another woman came along, who was probably an acquaintance of the crying one. She grabbed her by the elbow and asked:

"What's happened to you, Marina?"

The woman looked about and began wailing again:

"You see, I went out to Nura's flat, just for a minute,

to borrow some oil, and I ordered my parasite: 'Don't go anywhere, I haven't got my keys!' But he slipped away and slammed the door shut, and it locked! Couldn't he grasp that the clothes iron was turned on? The brainless fool! On Saturdays he can't think of anything but drinking his fill. Oh, the fire will be over the whole street! Oh, dear me! There are newspapers next to it — it'll be like kindling...."

"Well, it's clear now," said the fat man to the women. "Her husband's run away, she hasn't got the keys and the iron is on. How careless of you to leave the house without turning the electrical appliances off."

"I went out just for a minute. If I had known he could do it!" responded Marina dejectedly and sniveled again, without turning her head.

"Wait," said her acquaintance, "But your Vitya might have turned the iron off."

Marina burst out again:

"And pigs might fly! He never turns anything off, the lazy lizard! I wish he were poisoned with his vodka, the tipsy mug! If we've started a fire we will be paying out for it all our lives!"

"It's all clear then," said the fat man, "it could end up with a fire."

"Then, I guess, it makes sense to call for the fire-brigade, and immediately," responded the tall man.

But the other onlookers said that if the iron had, in fact, been turned off, it would be a false alarm, and the woman would indeed be in real trouble.

"Look, there's no fire so far. If there were, we'd see smoke from the transom. It's open."

Everybody looked up. Over the first floor, made of brick, there were two wooden stories, decorated with patterned cornices. Within a large window group in the upper story, a smaller window, known as a transom, was gaping wide open, like a black square among the other reflective panes.

The two girls, who stood at the gate when Maxim jumped, came up to the house too. They looked at the transom and quickly understood what had happened. One girl said:

"If only somebody could climb up there and turn the

iron off...."

"Well, I think that's a very sound idea," said the tall man. "But who'll take the risk? There's a knack to it."

Maybe they were saying it for no particular reason, but Maxim felt as if cool hairy beetles started running under his shirt. Who could have a knack for it? Of course, it was not that fat man or the old women with their bags. And not the girls, with their mouths foolishly open.

Probably, they had already seen the concert on TV and now remembered how he sang about the flight.

But singing and climbing are not the same thing. It was about seven meters up to that window with the transom: if he tumbled down he wouldn't land in one piece.... But what about his pilot's field cap? And besides, it was him who sang "I am not afraid of heights at all." After that just try and pretend that it wasn't your business and walk away! Maybe the people would say nothing, but he knew the way they would look at him....

And after that how would he feel himself, wearing his field cap with the little wings?

Maxim looked at the drainpipe. It was even impossible to say that it was old and fragile; or, that it was rusty and he would get dirty. As ill luck would have it, the drainpipe was new, firm and was covered with brown oil paint.

But he climbed up the pole in the school gymnasium and never fell....

And, to tell the truth, it would be great if he saved the house from fire in sight of all these people....

With a sinking heart, Maxim took off his field cap and put the boltik into it. Then he unbuttoned his waistcoat, took it off and held everything out to the tall man:

"Keep these a minute, please."

The man respectfully took Maxim's belongings. The other onlookers started talking to each other:

"Ooh, what a brave lad...."

"It'll be all right, he's as light as a feather; he'll be there in the blink of an eye."

"Light as a feather! If only his mother could see him...."

"We'll catch him if he falls...."

"Listen, boy, the main thing is, don't be afraid; just

forget that it's high...."

"Comrades, why are you letting him? What if something goes wrong?"

"But a fire could start at any moment!"

"Boy, don't do it!"

"Don't do it!" It was too late to retreat now. Without looking round, Maxim went up to the drainpipe. He took off his sandals and socks and looked up, along the drainpipe. The people around probably saw how he was deft, supple and quick as he was going to take the risk. Somebody stepped heavily behind him — it was the fat man.

"Acrobat, let me help you a bit. It'll be easier for you."

And before Maxim had time to take a breath he was two meters up, almost at the level of the first floor.

He clung to the drainpipe, gripped it with his knees, feet and palms, pressed into it with his chest and even with his cheek. As if he was glued to it. He looked down. Everybody looked at him in expectation. Maxim sighed and started climbing up....

Although the drainpipe was new, it was not slippery; at the same time it was not scratchy and it virtually stuck to his legs and palms. The corner of the house was in the shade; the drainpipe had not warmed up in the sun and it was pleasantly cool. Maxim pressed against it with his cheek after every movement up. It dispelled his fear.

In short, it wasn't too difficult to climb up, and Maxim realized that soon he would get to the level of the third floor.

But what should he do next?

He pulled himself up one last time and stood on the crosspiece that secured the drainpipe to the wall. It was narrow and hurt his feet. Maxim clenched his teeth, hissed with pain and, as soon as he could, stepped on the long narrow ledge that separated the third and the second stories.

The open transom window was the third from the corner. Clutching at the window frames and prominent decorations, he edged forward along the wall. It became rather frightening again, and to prevent his trembling Maxim began persuading himself that things were not frightening at all; the ground was just two stories below, even one and a half because the first brick story was a basement rather than a real story. And if something went wrong, the fat man had promised to catch him....

At last, he reached the window. He tried opening the sash windows, but of course they were locked. The most difficult part of his way was still ahead. The people below were arguing, giving advice and even insisting he to climb down. But he didn't pay attention to them. He knew that there was only one way forward — to get into the flat through the transom.

Holding onto the lower edge of the transom, he stood up on the narrow windowsill. The edge was now level with his chest. Maxim put his head and shoulders through the transom and hung over the window sash, skimming his knees over the slippery glass. In this way, he managed to squeeze himself more and more inside. Finally he leaned over and fell headlong into the room with a cry of victory.

And he was just in time! The room was already full of acrid smoke. The iron lay on its cast-iron stand, but the stand had heated and the woolen blanket under it was already smoldering.

Maxim pulled the plug out of the socket, took the iron and struck it against the stand. The stand rolled across the room and landed near the door. Now that the iron was safe; Maxim placed it on the stand. Then, coughing with the smell of burnt wool, he went to the window, unlocked it and opened it. The people were staring at him from below, with their mouths open wide.

"It's all right!" said Maxim. "I've turned it off. There really could have been fire soon. The blanket was already smoldering."

He was reserved, but his soul was rejoicing. The two girls glanced at each other and, all of a sudden, started applauding as though it was a concert. And then the other people, the adults, began clapping too. They all clapped — the fat man, and the women (who had put their bags on the pavement), and the tall man in glasses (he had hung Maxim's waistcoat over his forearm), and even the big boys who had arrived when Maxim was climbing into the transom.

Maxim moved half a step from the window and blushed a little. For the second time today he was rewarded with applause. He was a victor again. Maybe he was wrong when he thought he was a coward?

Trying not to show his confusion, Maxim leant over the windowsill again. He needed to ask how to get out of the flat. But he did not even have time to ask. Loud-voiced Marina, who was the only person who didn't applaud, shouted to him:

"Boy, now go to the corridor and unlock the door. I am coming upstairs!"

And she minced into the yard, her figure resembling a blue walking stick with a checkered knob.

Through the kitchen Maxim came to the corridor. It was illuminated by a yellow electric light bulb and smelt, for some reason, of rust and kerosene. On a wall hung a big iron trough, a bicycle without the front wheel and some old coats. The big door, with a wooden carving, was fitted with a shiny, new lock. It was very complicated, with many levers and buttons. Just like on a real safe! Maxim tried to press and pull some of them but without any result. Then he heard hurried small steps.

"How can I get it open?" asked Maxim impatiently. "I am late for school."

"There is a little button on the bottom, press it, then draw aside a little lever and pull it...."

There were two buttons on the lock. Maxim pressed each of them in turn, then all together and he pulled the levers. The lock was resisting with iron stubbornness. Maxim struck it with his fist and hurt the joint of his little finger. With his finger in his mouth he lisped:

"Whath a shyshtem! I'm thelling you, it doeshn't open!"

"Oh, it's stuck!" wailed Marina. "It always sticks if the door slammed hard!"

Maxim pulled his finger out of his mouth and demanded angrily:

"Then, go and call for a locksmith. I must go to school. It's time."

"Where can I find him on Saturday? Wait until my Vitya comes!"

Argh, who knew when her Vitya would come back!

Success always adds strength. Maxim felt an angry boldness. Resolutely striding in his bare feet he went to the window again. After all it was even better — to come down by the same risky way.

"Her lock is jammed," explained Maxim loudly to the onlookers below, with a note of scorn. "And I have to go to school."

He deftly climbed over the windowsill and stood on the narrow ledge again.

"Boy!" said the man who wore glasses. "Don't do it! No need to risk your neck now, but you—"

But he didn't finish. There was no point because Maxim was already on his way to the drainpipe. He was edging along the wall quickly and tenaciously. His shirt came untucked from his waistband and was fluttering in the light wind, probably looking as fine as Batman's cloak. Maxim was not afraid. The way was familiar, going down was certainly easier than climbing up — he would be down in no time. One time his hand lost its grip, and the girls gasped loudly. But it only added Maxim's courage. He grabbed hold of the drainpipe, looked down and began descending again. The fat man came nearer and spread his arms wide.

"Thank you, I'll manage myself," said Maxim. He slipped down and stepped on the drainpipe bend, which was a half- meter from the ground.

At this moment the angle pipe broke off the wall brackets and crashed to the ground. Together with Maxim.

He tumbled down on his side, on his shoulder and elbow, and was then thrown against the basement, striking its rough bricks with his left knee.

For a second he lay stunned. Then he thought: "Oh, how foolish! To tumble down almost standing on the ground. Enough to make a cat laugh." He quickly sat up and looked at his elbow: was his shirt very torn? Strange, but it was all intact, and not even dirty. Good!

With his hands he pushed himself up from the

ground, to stand and laugh together with all the people. But his knee hurt as if a shell had burst it into a hundred prickly splinters! Maxim gasped and looked at his knee. There was something red and glistening. Maxim closed his eyes tight, and felt sick.

People crowded round him trying to support him.

"Careful, be careful! Are you hurt badly, boy?" (They shouldn't ask questions like that! His knee is throbbing with pain, and he can barely check his tears.)

"Quiet, comrades. Don't touch his leg, it might be broken!" (That'll be the last straw! The Pioneer meeting is the day after tomorrow!)

"We must call for an ambulance. They'll put stitches in...." (Mama! What stitches is he talking about?)

"No, no need for any stitches, any cuts on boys heal up in no time...." (That's another matter.)

"Don't say that! Look at the dirt in it! What if he gets an infection? He needs a vaccination...."

"No, I don't!" said Maxim desperately.

"Calm down, boy, don't worry. We need to bandage your cut. Does anybody have a clean handkerchief?" (What a pity, his kerchief remained at home.)

"Girls, do you have a handkerchief? No? And you are called 'girls'?"

"There's a hospital not far away. We'll carry him there!" (These are the big boys. It's no problem for them! They'll pick him up and carry him. And once he's there....)

"Be quiet, comrades. Where is he injured? Let me see him."

It was a deep, commanding voice. Maxim unstuck his wet eyelids.

Through the tears still hanging on his eyelashes, he saw a huge man.

The man was huge both in height and in width. He was like a tower. A tower dressed in the blue uniform of a civil pilot, and his white uniform cap loomed somewhere in the clouds. His exterior was extraordinary too. It seemed that the pilot consisted of big, round folds. His vast stomach was in folds, skin-tight in the uniform jacket; his neck and big face were in folds, too. And from there, from that height, his very blue eyes looked at

Maxim genially and intently. They were like the eyes of the carpenter who had presented Maxim with the gold chip.

The people stepped aside. The man-tower pulled out a snow-white handkerchief from his trouser pocket and squatted down over Maxim, his folds stirred. Then he resolutely took Maxim's leg in his big hands....

The handkerchief was the size of a small tablecloth. The tight bandage pressed, weakening the pain; the fear had gone away. The pilot helped Maxim to stand up.

"Can you stand on your foot?"

Maxim tried and said in a whisper:

"I can, if not hard."

He wiped his eyelashes with his sleeve, blinked and asked:

"Where's my field cap?"

The tall man hurriedly approached:

"Here you are, please. And your screw is here too."

Maxim smiled:

"It's my boltik."

The people helped him on with his little waistcoat, pulled his socks on and buckled up his sandals. The pilot saw his field cap and boomed:

"Aha, I see that you're an aviator. So, you've had a crash landing?"

Maxim smiled again, looked at his knee and suddenly felt his fear coming back: on the handkerchief a red spot appeared. The pilot said to the crowd:

"My car's over there. I'll take this wounded fellow to our medical unit. They'll know what to do with him."

The adult onlookers started talking animatedly with each other; they were glad that things went well.

Of course, there was no problem for them. It was not they, but Maxim who would be carried away to the medical unit, where all sorts of glassy things were on the shelves: forceps, scissors, syringes....

"Maybe there's no need? It'll heal up itself," he said pitifully.

The pilot muttered something in a low, bear-like voice, took Maxim like a small chip and carried him along the street. There was simply no way to escape from his bear paws.

On the other hand, maybe everything would be all right. They might bandage him and let him go. Vaccination would probably not be necessary....

Maxim calmed a little. Comfortably rocking, as though he was in a cradle, he was floating over the sidewalk. The pilot smelt of strong cologne and tobacco. He had gray eyebrows, tufted light hair and a big, round nose covered with a faint network of small veins. His eyes looked very kind. It suddenly occurred to Maxim that the pilot looked like Santa Claus who had been shaved and dressed in a uniform.

The pilot had carried Maxim to his old, well-worn car and put him in the front seat. Then he went round the car and began squeezing himself in. The car groaned and sank on its springs.

"Yeah, it's no fun getting old...," the pilot said and looked at Maxim with some confusion. Then he asked anxiously: "Does it hurt? Try not to bend your leg for a while."

Maxim glanced at his knee and shortly sighed: the red blot had become bigger.

The pilot quickly began pressing the starter. The car started juddering.

"Just wait, we'll get there in a jiffy...."

"Where?"

"Do you know where the flight-control building is? It's right over there."

"Yes, of course I know! Nearby there's the Culture Palace. I sing in the chorus there. Look, this is our uniform, and our chorus is called 'The Little Wings'."

"That's great," said the pilot in his deep voice. "I realized at once that you're a man like me, from aviation— And how did you happen to land so amiss?"

"Ah, well, it's because of this woman," explained Maxim jauntily. "Her husband left and locked the door, and her electric iron was turned on. I had to climb up to the third story. It was good that I was just in time: it was starting to burn...."

"Aha, I see you're a hero."

Maxim's ears became warm, and he turned his face to the window. The car had started, and soon the familiar houses of Titov Street began flitting by.

"Now, we'll get there in no time," the pilot spoke soothingly. "They'll repair you quickly. You need to have your cut washed and bandaged.... Well, a little jab in one place won't be bad, either; nobody's lived to grow old without one. And soon you'll be as good as new."

"But, maybe a jab is not necessary?" Maxim responded in a weak voice.

"No, my old fellow, it is. There's no need for foolish risks. When I was at the front, in 1945, there was a flight engineer in my plane. All through the war he had passed safe and sound, and then he cut his hand, dirtied his wound and died. On the twelfth day he was all stiff with tetanus. So, it's better to do the right thing."

That was it. There was no hope. Even if Maxim had a chance to run away, he would not do it now. To have a jab is terrible of course, yet dying when you haven't even lived as much as ten years is worse. Especially when you have so many victories under your belt and summer is around.

Chapter five

RESENTMENT

The car stopped near the flight control building, at a side entrance. The pilot got out (making the car give a creaking sigh) and opened the door on Maximka's side. Looking at him with smiling eyes he held out his big palms.

"Well, pilot, come to my hands?"

The affair was coming to a head. Maxim felt a cold emptiness and the taut strings of his anxiety were moaning there in a monotonous and repugnant way. It was exactly what is known as fear. And with this feeling your legs become weak even if they are both safe and sound.

But besides fear, any human being has pride. It fights against fear, and they try to pin each other down. Inside

Maxim there was still no winner. He started getting out of the car.

"I'll go myself."

"Does it hurt, your leg?"

Maxim carefully put his weight on his left foot. Pain pricked his knee, but it was bearable. It was nothing compared with the things that were ahead.

"No, it doesn't. I can walk," he said despondently.

"Good for you!"

They went through the little garden and came up to the blue door with a red cross on it. Yes, life is a strange thing! When you are afraid of something it works like a magnet for the trouble you are trying to evade.

He remembered the pilot's words about "one place" and assured himself that it's probably is less painful than an injection under the shoulder blade. Although on the other hand, it is more unpleasant.... But surely, the doctors in a medical unit for pilots are men. That was better....

In the cool corridor there was a row of white doors. The pilot went up to the farthest. Maxim limped behind him. The taut strings inside him stopped moaning, but the shaky emptiness remained.

The medical unit looked exactly as Maxim had expected. On the glassy shelves there were bandages, vials and a multitude of glittering things. There were also some chairs and a couch covered with oilcloth.

But instead of a man, the doctor was a girl. She wore the same doctor's coat and cap as the school nurse, Svetlana Sergeevna. She was very young. She raised her thin eyebrows and asked with a smile:

"Ah, Ivan Savelyevich! Glad to see you. What's happened now?"

"Nothing's happened to me, Lubushka," responded the pilot, and from his deep voice something tinkled on the glassy shelves. "Here you are, I've brought you a wounded pilot. This guy's just had a bad landing...."

He stepped aside and showed Maxim, who was staying behind his mighty back.

"Aye-aye!" the nurse exclaimed again. "It's your grandson, Ivan Savelyevich, isn't it?"

"For heaven's sake, Lubushka! I've got a granddaughter, Natashka. And this is our man, from the aviation. Just look at his field cap. So, come on, and mend this fine young man quickly."

"Yes, now I see," Luba replied and met with Maxim's eyes. Her eyes were cheerful and merry. But Maxim's mood was far from fun, and he looked away. Luba drew near, held him fast under his armpits and deftly seated him on the couch. The oilcloth on the couch was cold. Maxim flinched. Luba hurriedly asked:

"What's wrong, little one? Afraid?"

"Not at all," answered Maxim in a hollow voice.

"Well, that's good then!"

She had undone the handkerchief on his knee, quickly unwound it and carefully took it off.

"Gosh.... You did your best as I see.... But well, there's actually nothing terrible, it's only nasty to look at. You've just scratched it badly, that's all."

Maxim looked at his knee from the corner of his eye, blinked and began looking through the window. There, an orange helicopter was slowly descending right on the grassy field.

Luba came up to the glass cabinet and started clinking with bottles. She took a bottle, cotton pads and headed for Maxim again.

"Don't be afraid, it's not iodine and it won't sting."

Maxim only moved his shoulder. Let it be a hundred bottles of iodine! It's not a syringe with an implacable, thin needle.

The liquid from the bottle was hissing like fizzy water and cooled the skin. Then his leg was tightly dressed with a bandage. He felt hardly any pain.

Maxim looked at Luba with hope: "Maybe that's all?" But she opened the glass cabinet again and took out a nickel-plated box. Maxim could see the helicopter reflected on its side as an orange glimpse. Then there appeared a syringe.

Ivan Savelyevich was sitting at the door. The small white stool looked very tiny under him. He looked at Maxim with sympathy. Then he winked: "It's all right, bear up!"

Luba turned to Maxim.

"Now she'll say 'take your shorts off,'" he thought drearily and recollected that recently he was in the cinema and saw a movie where a big guy had got into an accident and then ran away from the hospital when they wanted to give him a shot. The audience laughed very much then. But what could Maxim, a small boy, do?

But Luba was a good nurse. She said:

"Undo your shirt-sleeve, please."

Maxim tried to undo the button on his cuff, but his fingers disobeyed.

Luba bent over him and asked in a whisper:

"Are you afraid?"

It was no use telling a lie, and Maxim said with a short sigh:

"A little bit...."

"Don't worry, I'll do it quickly, you won't even notice. Look aside and count to three."

Maxim felt the cool of the spirit sodden cotton pad.... He took a deep breath through his clenched teeth—

Oh dear! How is it possible not to notice such things! He squeezed the boltik in his fist so hard that it almost skewered his palm with its head.

"There! there! Now that's all. Good for you!"

That's all? She said, "That's all!" The end!!

The end to a foul fear! No need to shrivel and flinch any more! All of a sudden Maxim got angry. Why was he such a coward? Why was he afraid up to the point of sickness? Was it because of just one second? "Count to three...." He did not even have time to. Well, it was painful but just for a moment. And how much had he suffered from fear? A thousand times more than from the jab. A fool and a sop! And he imagined that he was Batman!

"Don't pull down your shirt-sleeve, let it get dry," said Luba tenderly.

Maxim nodded and carefully shifted his weight onto his bandaged leg. And he smiled. However angry he was, his joy was stronger. The joy that his fear remained behind. And ahead was the day resembling a festival.... And from this day he would never be afraid any more. Now he knew how foolish it was to flinch because of a mere trifle.

Ivan Savelyevich stood up too — with sighs and noise, but quickly. He resembled the birth of a new island, which was rising from the ocean depths.

"Well, Lubushka, I'll take this fellow and deliver him to his home. OK?"

Luba looked at Ivan Savelyevich undecidedly, and at Maxim, a bit guiltily.

"That's not all... I've vaccinated the boy with a kind of serum that must not be injected in full dose right away. So, in an hour we shall have to repeat the injection."

Probably she saw Maxim's pitiful eyes and added hurriedly:

"You can sit in our garden or have a walk. You can even see how the planes fly. This hour will fly by quickly.... What's your name?"

"Maxim," he said in a whisper and turned his face to the door.

He felt as if he had been presented with a wonderful present, and in a moment it was taken away. To make fun of him....

Ivan Savelyevich took Maxim's shoulder with his huge palm — Maxim felt as if a saddle was put on him.

"We'll wait together. Anyway, I've nowhere to hurry off to; I am on leave. We'll sit and talk. Let's go to the garden, Maxim."

Maxim limped to the door. Then along the corridor. A bitter disappointment was eating him away. Maxim even struck the wall furtively with his fist holding the boltik. Because the vexation was biting and... without fear.

Maxim felt himself with surprise, that there was no fear. Well almost, there was a tiny remainder.... Why? Maybe because he hadn't known about the second vaccination and had spent all his supply of fear on the first one?

They walked out into the garden and sat down on a bench made of wooden planks. Maxim felt his nerves once more. Every centimeter of them. Maybe his fear had hidden itself somewhere? What if it leaped out again and caught him? No! There was nothing, indeed. His heart was beating evenly and easy.

Of course, the remaining shot did not make him glad, but now Maxim felt neither sickening weakness nor trembling. It was only a pity that he had to wait a whole hour. It would be good to have it right now. Maxim would not even turn pale. Maybe only just a bit....

So that was the end? No need now to flinch when you hear sudden steps in the school corridor. No need to fear that sly Mishka Stremenenko would suspect your cowardice and tell the whole class!

These thoughts dispelled his vexation. And again he felt that joy had returned. The composed joy of a brave man.

Behind the garden fence there was a long wooden building with thin aerials and a high mast. A thick "sausage", which resembled a long butterfly net, was fluttering in the warm wind. It was made for the pilots so they could see the wind direction when they are coming in to land.

The planes landed and took off regularly. There were a lot of them: small silvery passenger planes with blue stripes, motley sporting airplanes and helicopters that looked like multicolored dragonflies. All the air was filled with the vibration of their engines. Maxim thought it looked as though he had entered a magic country inhabited by huge grasshoppers.

The field was barred by the garden fence, and Maxim climbed onto the high back of the bench. Then he remembered that his sandals were dirty and hurriedly kicked them off on the grass: the bench was recently painted with shiny sky-blue paint.

Maxim stole a look at Ivan Savelyevich, but he apparently didn't notice anything. He took his uniform cap off and sat looking at the planes. From his perch Maxim saw his huge shoulders, shoulder straps with wide gold bars and his thin gray locks through which pink skin was seen.

A big red and yellow helicopter flew over them at a very low height. It cast a shadow, and it even seemed that from its sparkling screw had come a breath of cool air.

Ivan Savelyevich glanced at Maxim, and they both

smiled. As though they were both pilots and understood each other without saying a word.

And Maxim wanted very much to be related, at least a bit, to this motley, winged life. He could not help it and said:

"Today we appeared on television. I sang the song about the first flight. Did you see the concert this morning?"

"No, I didn't," said Ivan Savelyevich regretfully, "What a pity! If only I had known about it! Especially since I wasted that time. I came to the office to put in an application for my vacation but forgot that it's closed on Saturdays."

"Do you work here?" asked Maxim, to keep up the conversation.

"Yes, I do.... Recently I tried to retire, but couldn't. Even if I can't fly, I want to be near the planes, closer to my friends."

"And which planes did you fly?" asked Maxim gingerly.

"Me? Maximchik, I flew many kinds of planes, but mostly the passenger ones. During the war I was a navigator in the north and I flew heavy bombers.... And before the war, you won't even believe me, I flew an airship several times."

"An airship?" gasped Maxim. "Was it like in the film 'Engineer Garin's Hyperboloid'?"

"Yes, but it was bigger."

"And these?" Maxim nodded, watching a little green training plane that flashed over their heads.

"That goes without saying.... It's only now I can barely get into my car — there was a time when I was slim, I can't even believe it, just like you."

Maxim laughed. He imagined Ivan Savelyevich as a scrawny little boy in his cherry-colored uniform (Maximka's), but with his real head — big and gray, with the white cap. Ivan Savelyevich grinned too.

"Well.... And now I can fly only as a passenger. Although, the doctors don't recommend even that."

"It's because your heart isn't well?" asked Maxim knowingly.

"Nobody knows what's wrong with me.... I've got a poor heart, liver, spleen and lots of other things too.... Do you know, Maxim, I am very old."

"No, not very," argued Maxim politely.

"It is true, my old fellow. My eldest grandson is already flying. And my youngest granddaughter's like you, perhaps just a little older. She became a Pioneer recently."

"I will too, the day after tomorrow," said Maxim jealously. "There has already been a meeting, and they decided to admit me. I would have been admitted before, but I started that school just recently."

"I expect they wanted to know you better, first...," remarked Ivan Savelyevich.

"Yes, probably. But now that's all decided. Now everyone in my class will be Pioneers. Except Tylikov."

"Tylikov? Wait, it's a somewhat familiar surname.... Ah, no, that man was Tupikov. He was a navigator when I worked in Dixon. But who's this Tylikov? Is he such a great villain?"

Maxim shrugged his shoulders.

"No, he isn't. But he does behave badly, and he argues with Sofia Iosifna all the time. Once, he brought a catapult to school, and he jumps about during breaks."

"Well," said Ivan Savelyevich in a strange tone. "That is of course.... Although, my Natashka also likes hopping. And what are his other sins?"

"Well, in general... Sofia Iosifna said that he was disobedient."

"Well, old friend, what a characterization! But what do 'obedient' and 'disobedient' mean? It's unclear."

Maxim wondered:

"Why is it unclear?"

"Well, look for yourself. Let's take our pilots, for instance. They are given characterizations, too. If a person is good they write: able, competent, brave, disciplined.... Can you imagine them writing: 'obedient pilot', 'disobedient navigator'?"

Maxim blinked several times in surprise. But indeed, it sounded like rubbish.

"But pilots... they are grown-ups. And we are not, yet...."

"I see that you are not," remarked Ivan Savelyevich in a slightly angry voice. "But people must learn how to be adult while they are small; after that it's too late. I'm telling my Natashka this all the time...."

It seemed he was right. Of course he was right! Ivan Savelyevich was not a man who could deceive. But it was so unusual....

"But you said 'disciplined,'" recalled Maxim. "Isn't that the same thing as 'obedient'?"

"How do you make that out!" argued Ivan Savelyevich. "Disciplined — it's when a person knows what he has to do, sees what's going on around him, carries out orders and can order himself if necessary. He can quickly make a decision, doesn't let his friends down and doesn't do stupid things.... Discipline, it's when a person answers to himself for his own deeds. But what is an obedient man? Is he brave? It isn't known. Could he leave his friend in trouble? Who knows? Will he lose his head in danger? That's unclear, too. Can he work? Where would you go to find out? A sheep also can be obedient, my boy. And a man must be able to fight for the truth. Understand?"

"Yes, I do," replied Maxim. He wanted to say that in general Tylikov never scuffled with anybody; only once had he beaten up a strong fourth grader who had cut a fine gold braid off Svetka Meshalkina's coat.

But he didn't. He saw that ill-fated Marina coming from the garden wicket-gate, straight towards them. That very woman, whose iron could start a fire.

What did she need here?

Maybe she had remembered an untapped faucet or a gas-stove and was going to ask Maxim to climb up into her flat again? Not on her life!

"That's good, very well," said Marina. "I almost ate my heart out, but the neighbors said where you'd gone, and I ran after you."

Maxim turned slightly pink. It was clear that Marina recollected that she had not thanked her rescuer, and she had now come running especially for that. Maybe she was going to offer him a reward? What next! He didn't need it....

"Boy," Marina nearly sang it in a sweet voice, "I came

for my money. Give it back to me and everything will be OK. Don't be afraid, we won't say anything to your mother and father. It's so easy to take a wrong step at your age."

"What?" said Maxim, dumbfounded.

"Yes, the money that was on the table. Where is it? You've taken it! Well, confess quickly to taking it and give it back. My salary's much less than a pilot's...."

"Madam, are you crazy?" said Maxim loudly and stood up on the bench. The pain shot through his knee, but he immediately forgot about it. He felt suddenly that it was ridiculous. Most ridiculous. And, laughing, he explained:

"There wasn't any money there! There was only a burnt blanket."

"Don't laugh at an adult!" Marina began speaking in a different tone. "The money couldn't fly out the window by itself. And there's no reason I should lose my five rubles!"

"What, do you think I am a thief?" calmly asked Maxim and looked at Ivan Savelyevich: his face had a deadpan expression and he was looking not at Maxim but at Marina.

"I tell you, I have nothing!" cried Maxim. "What nonsense! I haven't even got any pockets, look!"

He pulled the buttons, thrust open his little waistcoat and turned around on his unhurt leg.

"See? Where have I put your money? Have I eaten it up? Where?"

And suddenly he fell silent, as though from the sound of a shot. Only there was no shot, but an awful thought: "The breast pocket! There, there are Mama's five rubles!"

Neither the fear he felt because of vaccination, nor any of his other fears could be compared with that horror. What could he do now? How could he prove it?

"Ivan Savelyevich," he said helplessly, "I have only this.... But it's mine...."

(Just a moment before he said he had nothing, not even pockets — and then!)

"This is mine, honestly.... I forgot. My mama gave it to me for lunch...."

(But who gives children so much money for lunch?)

Maxim didn't care about foolish Marina. But Ivan Savelyevich! What was he thinking of him now?

Maxim pulled out the five ruble bank note from the pocket and held it out to him.

"Look, that's my mama's! Word of honor! I didn't take it...."

Ivan Savelyevich looked at him in surprise and, it seemed, with compassion.

Marina snatched the money.

"Well, well! 'I didn't take it!'"

She put the blue bank note up to her sharp nose, as if she wanted to sniff at it.

"It seems, it's not mine, that one was soiled.... I guess he's changed it in some shop.... Or, it's my Vitka who grabbed it... I say, tell the truth, where did you take it?"

Ivan Savelyevich sighed noisily and began to get up from the bench with a strained face.

"I didn't take it!" desperately repeated Maxim. "Ivan Savelyevich, I say, I am telling the truth! If you like, let's go to my home, I live not far, and my mama will tell you! I live not far...."

"Calm, calm down, lad," said Ivan Savelyevich.

With his two fingers he took the money from Marina's hand and put it carefully into Maxim's little pocket. He was looking at Marina from head to toe. And, although she was tall, she now seemed somehow shorter.

"Madam," said Ivan Savelyevich with a frown, "look back, please. Over there. Can you see that wicket-gate? Go through it and close it from the other side. This is the airport service area. I'll call for the officer of the watch if you need help."

"What, what?" Marina said in a clucking way. "What's going on? The officer of the watch? Call him, I don't care. And you don't scare me; I've seen a lot of the likes of you. I'll go and call the police myself. There's no getting away from swindlers!"

The mighty neck of Ivan Savelyevich had turned cherry colored, as Maxim's field cap. He took a deep, gurgling breath and bellowed:

"SSSCAT!"

Maxim bent down as if he got under a squall. A flock of frightened sparrows rushed from the control center roof and noisily flew off. Marina was swept at least three meters away. There she turned around and quickly minced to the wicket. It looked like a funny cartoon in which a tall man with short legs eluded the dog's pursuit. His legs outran his body; he was running with his back bent, but he didn't fall over.

Ivan Savelyevich followed Marina with his eyes till she disappeared behind the corner. Then he rubbed his neck and looked at Maxim with a scowl.

"Can't understand you...."

Maxim stood before him on the bench, frightened and puzzled.

"I don't understand," said Ivan Savelyevich. "You're not guilty. And if you're not guilty, why are you in a flap and trembling like a rabbit? A man must have dignity, but you justify yourself like a petty thief. If you're in the right, what are you afraid of?"

"I wasn't afraid of her. I was afraid that you... would think...."

Ivan Savelyevich took Maxim by his elbows and carefully drew him closer.

"Maxim, Maxim, what a young head.... I've lived seven decades. Is it possible that I can't distinguish a good man from a swindler? Well, you are a little heron.... Oh, Maxim, what's up? Oh, well, no... no need for this."

Of course, there was no reason for it, but what could Maxim do? Maybe from the unexpected hug, or maybe because of all his recent feelings, he burst into tears and began to shake, pressing himself into Ivan Savelyevich as if against a cliff.

"Aye-aye...," said Ivan Savelyevich. "Now that's enough, Maxim. You'll wet me through."

"If I'd known, I'd never have climbed up there...," murmured Maxim to somehow diminish his embarrassment.

Ivan Savelyevich sat down, took Maxim up and put him on his lap.

"Oh, don't speak like that! Does that foolish woman matter at all? You were saving a whole house where many people live...."

From shame Maxim's tears had at once turned off. And putting the boltik first in one hand then in the other, he started angrily rubbing his face with his palms. And he forgot that his left palm was sweaty and dirty because of the boltik.

"Oho, you've decorated yourself like a Red Indian from a book. Come on!"

He led Maxim out of the garden to the edge of the airfield. In the grass there an iron pipe with a copper tap was sticking up.

Ivan Savelyevich took a big handful of water, and in two movements he washed all the dirty stripes from Maxim's face. Maxim sniffed angrily.

"There's nothing to wipe you with," murmured Ivan Savelyevich. "I left my handkerchief in Lubushka's room."

Maxim sniffed once more, pulled his shirt out of his waistband and quickly wiped his face.

"Ah, a masterstroke!" approved Ivan Savelyevich. "Well, now we're going to go to Lubushka, aren't we, Maxim — the hero?"

"The hero!" repeated Maxim with angry despair. "If you want to know, I am a coward.... And probably a show-off, too."

"Why?" wondered Ivan Savelyevich.

Because he was so angry with himself, Maxim was ready to explain everything: about the vaccinations, about Transistor, and the reason he climbed up to turn off that iron. But it was difficult, and he could not find the words. He frowned and answered:

"Probably I was born like that."

"No, you weren't. I say, you are a good boy, you are!"

He probably thought that Maxim was ashamed because of his recent tears and said:

"It doesn't matter that you cried. It happens sometimes when a person feels hurt. When I was twenty-four, the chief of our bomber squadron shouted at me for no reason. I was big and strong, but I burst into tears like a girl. I remember it even now.... The chief even got scared, and began to console me...."

Maxim smiled, although from time to time he still shuddered from his recent tears. And when they came to the medical unit, Luba noticed that.

"Maxim, have you been crying? Did it hurt you so

much? This time I'll do it more carefully, don't be afraid, my little one."

"I'm not afraid at all," said Maxim gloomily.

"There's another reason. Resentment," explained Ivan Savelyevich. "But, in general, that's all over."

Maxim almost indifferently glanced at the thin jet that spouted from the needle. And, wondering at his composure, he held his hand out.

His joy was gradually returning. After all, he had saved the house anyway. And his boastful thoughts... well! Next time he would be wiser. But he didn't chicken out. And was not afraid now— Ouch! But he was not afraid anyway....

Maxim stood up and waved his hand, to dry the vaccination place more quickly.

"Drop in to see me on Monday, I'll change the bandage and write you a medical certificate for the vaccination. It's so you won't be vaccinated if you get another cut. But I haven't got the stamp now," said Luba. "Deal?"

"Deal!" Maxim agreed with a smile.

"He will, he will," promised Ivan Savelyevich. "He'll drop in to see me, too. I'll introduce him to my granddaughter."

When they got into the car Ivan Savelyevich asked:

"Where am I taking you? You said your home's nearby."

"Could you take me up to the school? We've got an excursion now."

"Yes, no problem, but what about your leg?"

"But it doesn't hurt at all."

"Let's go."

In two minutes they were at the school.

"All right. Thank you, Ivan Savelyevich. I was thinking I'd be late."

"Maxim," said Ivan Savelyevich, "I say... if you'd like... drop around to my home. I've got a lot of plane models and photographs. I don't live far, in Gromov Street[1], house number 5, and my flat is five also. Remember?"

"Yes, I will! Thank you."

---

[1] *Mikhail Gromov, the famous Russian aviator (—Tr.)*

"Well, fly then, little heron...."

Chapter six

CINDERELLA

Yes, in one town there lived Cinderella. She lived at Gazetnaya Lane[1], not far from the high bank of the river. To tell the truth, she was not exactly the same as Cinderella from the fairy-tale. She didn't have a stepmother and evil sisters; she had a mother and grandmother, and they loved Cinderella very much.

And her real name was Tanya.

So why, then, was she Cinderella?

It was because her hands and face were often stained. It was not because of hard work (although she was not afraid of working hard), but because she was keen on mending her bicycle and painting things. The neighboring boys often asked her to decorate their shields, swords and arrow flights.

Another reason was that she was not very pretty, and she had been dreaming away all the time that a kind magician might one day make her a beauty.

Sometimes, when her mother and grandmother were out of the house, Tanya-Cinderella would go to a mirror and examine her face. Yes, there definitely wasn't anything peculiar about it. Her face was round and quite unsuited to her thin neck. As for her eyes, it was also hard to say whether they were blue or gray. And, probably, they were too far from the bridge of her nose. And her freckles.... If they were just normal freckles it would be all right, but they looked as though somebody started painting and then gave up: in one place there were several dots, but in another.... And her hair, too — it was not red, but a light ginger color. And it was disheveled because it suited neither for soft locks, nor heavy braids.

---

[1] *or Newspaper Lane*

That was why she had a short boyish haircut.

Tanya would put on her favorite dress, Mama's beads and Grandmother's lacy cloak, then decorate her head with a crown made of silver paper and twirl around the room. As if it was a ball in a king's palace.

However, she quickly tired of it.

First, whether you dance or not, it won't help you become a beautiful princess. Second, Tanya knew at heart that although she was not a beauty, on the whole she was rather attractive. A year ago, when she was a second grader, Yurka Voronihin remarked on it in a loud whisper to his neighbor, in a mathematics lesson. Tanya liked those words and remembered them. However, it didn't prevent her from reaching Yurka and whacking him with her textbook. Why did he say it? The big-eared prince!

The thing was, however, that Cinderella-Tanya had been dreaming of a real prince. She was Cinderella after all.

Her prince had to be slim, good-looking and brave. Kind and cheery. And he shouldn't resemble the boys she had known. They were all somewhat unsuitable — either timid or too cheeky. And they were worse chatterboxes than the girls. People like that can't keep secrets. They wouldn't even listen to her secrets. How could they understand that she was Cinderella? They could only imagine being heroes themselves.

Could they boast about something special? No, she could do everything they could do. She could ride a bicycle as well as they could, fence with swords, dive from rafts....

Tanya would take off the beads, the cloak, her trim dress and paper crown and pull on her jeans and sports shirt. While her prince couldn't be found, she had to be both Cinderella and the prince.

She would ride a bicycle, play football, hop with a skipping-rope, play scout and hopscotch, look after homeless kittens and, from time to time, she would fight. And sometimes she would go to her secret place at the riverbank and turn into the princess.

There she had everything: the palace, riches, secrets and weapons, soldiers and a court. To tell the truth, they were made of plasticine, but they looked good anyway.

But you cannot make a prince out of plasticine. He must be real.

Together they would go on travels, fight with the enemies and make discoveries. She would bandage his wounds and save him from any danger. Because, although princes are heroes, all the same they are boys, and you must constantly keep an eye on them....

That day Cinderella did not expect any miracles. She didn't even think of anything magical. All she thought about were simple things: weather to ride her bicycle or go to Yurka Voronihin and ask him for the book "The Girl From Earth." The book was about space and all kinds of adventures. Having thought it over, she decided that her bicycle would not run away, but Yurka might give the book to somebody else.

Yurka was not at home. Tanya felt slightly upset, but not very much, because the weather was so fine — the first really summery day. On a day like this, you simply couldn't be upset. In addition, tomorrow was Sunday and the holidays were going to begin very soon.

So Tanya kept going, not thinking of anything important, just looking around and— The fairy-tale arrived when it was not expected.

She saw her prince! He was going down the other side of the street, slight, slim and mysterious.

There was no doubt that he was her prince. Firstly, he was a stranger — Tanya knew all the local boys. Secondly, his raiment shone with a regal, dark-cherry color, and the buttons were glittering with gold. The only things he lacked were a lustrous cloak and thin sword. But he was fine even without them. His cherry-colored field cap was no worse in the least than a medieval plumed cap.

On his leg a fresh bandage displayed its whiteness, and his wounded leg probably hurt. He was trying not to limp and walked straight and confidently. It meant he had a strong character.

And his face was nice, too. Although Tanya had only caught a glimpse of it from some distance, she made it out at once.

Her heart stopped at first, and then started fluttering

in her chest, like a sparrow caught in a net. But Tanya took herself in hand.

Well, if a miracle has happened, you can't let it just walk off!

Tanya let the prince take forty steps and secretly followed him.

Chapter seven

JUNGLE AND DANGERS

When Maxim entered his class room he realized that he was late. The room was quiet and empty. The green school desks were shining under the sun rays like little glades. On the blackboard smiled a good-natured pirate in a striped jersey and jackboots — it had probably been chalked by Vladik Malashkin who often drew something like that. A wrapper from a "Kitty-kitty" toffee lay at the door. That was all.

Maxim felt a bit sad. Of course, nothing terrible had happened, but nevertheless.... All the class was having fun now, and he was here alone.

Maxim went out to the corridor. A distinct voice behind the next door was dictating a verse:

"I love thunder in the spring... I love thun-der... in the— Volkov, stop talking or I'll turn you out!... Write it down: in the spring...."

A second grader, who had been expelled from his class for his sins, was languishing by the window at the far end of the corridor. In the music room somebody was playing "In the Hall of the Mountain King" by Grieg, with one finger. Maxim liked that music. He wanted to come closer and listen to it, but suddenly he heard the clicking of somebody's heels and in the corridor appeared Anna Andreevna, head teacher of the primary classes. Maxim automatically stood straighter, pulled down his uniform and took off his field cap.

Anna Andreevna stopped and watchfully looked

around. She at once noticed the unhappy second grader who froze at the window. Then she saw Maxim. For a second she thought to whom she should go first. And she went toward Maxim.

"How do you do," said Maxim and smiled, just in case.

"I am interested to know, why are you here while the lesson's going on?" asked Anna Andreevna in a severe tone of voice, looking strictly at Maxim above her round glasses. She was tall and stout; under her left eyebrow there was a big mole, and when she moved her eyebrows it moved too. But why be afraid of her if you have done nothing wrong?

"My class went on an excursion, but I—"

"But you did not. May I ask why?"

"I knocked my leg on the way to school," said Maxim boldly and showed his bandaged knee. "I was taken to the hospital. They bandaged me up.... Then they gave me two shots. And I am late."

Somehow, imperceptibly, Anna Andreevna had turned from an exacting head-teacher into a big, kind woman.

"Oh, you poor thing," she said and even squatted down a little to examine the bandage. "Does your leg hurt?"

"Nope," said Maxim jauntily. "That is, it does hurt, but just a bit."

"Why didn't you go home?"

"It doesn't hurt much," repeated Maxim. "I wanted to go on the excursion, but everybody's already left. And I don't know where the park is."

"You don't know where the park is?" wondered Anna Andreevna.

"Yes. I've just recently moved to this town. I haven't been there, so far."

"Ah! You're Rybkin, from Class 3B," remembered Anna Andreevna. And she attentively looked over Maxim again. "What's the suit you're wearing? Is it the uniform from your previous school?"

"No, it's the choir 'The Little Wings.' This morning we appeared on television."

"Really? I see you're a celebrity! My congratulations. Now, the way to the park is simple. Our school is on Kirov

Street; so, take any tram as far as the 'Park' stop. It's close at hand, and the street goes along the river. The park is located on the riverbank. Can you get there by yourself?"

"Yes, I will. Thank you."

"You're welcome," Anna Andreevna smiled. "But be careful, don't cripple the other leg— How did you manage to hurt yourself so much?"

Maxim opened his mouth to explain jauntily how he had saved a house from fire, but Anna Andreevna had turned into the head teacher again. She straightened up and looked severely at the place where just now the second grader had been pining away. But he had already disappeared. Anna Andreevna adjusted her glasses and pursed her lips. Maxim saw that the conversation was over and said in a low voice:

"Goodbye."

When he came out into the street he thought, "If the park's near and on the bank, it's probably possible to get there on foot, along the river. Why jostle in a tram on such a great day? The river's a more interesting place."

Maxim had already been to the river in the spring, with his father, but then its banks were without grass, and the gray remains of ice floes were whirling in the water. The day then was overcast and windy. It was another matter today....

The bank of the river was four blocks from the school.

The bandage had loosened slightly, and his knee could bend almost freely. It would be hard to run, but it was not a long way to go.

The street had come down to the slope of the riverbank. Some time ago there had been a wooden fence along the bank, but now it was broken. Only the posts and crossbars remained.

Over the river, streets with wooden houses, pavements and some new blocks of flats could be seen. Two old churches stood right on the shore near the water. Under them there might be probably some secret passages and cellars with hidden treasures.

The river flowed broadly and freely. The water near

the shore was pale yellow, but farther on it reflected the sky and seemed quite blue. At the low bank opposite, the high water approached the houses and an orange excavator was working hastily trying to repair a clay dam.

Maxim was standing at the high bank and could see everything.

The bank was wonderful. It was as though a certain giant, in ancient times, had piled up huge lumps of soil and clay, mixed them together and sown into it all sorts of tall grass seeds.

If you could imagine that you were flying a plane, you could think that you saw mountains covered with jungle.

A kilometer away to the left, you could see a mass of trees, which looked like a green cloud. The park was probably there. Yes, of course! Its big, latticed Ferris wheel was visible above that green, as if the giant who had made this bank had probably forgotten his bicycle.

Small cabins were attached to the rim of the wheel. The wheel was rotating and the cabins flew around.

Maxim felt he wanted to run. The high bank was covered with fenced vegetable plots, but along the river slope some paths ran in all directions. The slope was overgrown with tall weeds, burdock and wormwood, and looked tempting and interesting. It was calling him, as a jungle thicket calls a hunter.

Maxim slid on his soles down the slippery slope to the nearest path, made a step and at once found himself standing in the grass up to his shoulders. There was a rustling silence and the smell of plants. It was a real thicket of young grass entangled with the gray stalks of last year's weeds, soft wormwood and dry hemp. Some lumps of clay got straight into his sandals, prickly seeds began falling down inside his collar and small hedgehogs of last year's burdock balls gladly seized him by his shorts and shirtsleeves. So what? Who said it would be easy? Maxim spread his elbows apart and bravely made his way through the grassy jungle.

The path leapt from one ledge to another; sometimes it dived into the dark drains where remains of snow still lay. But Maxim didn't stop to make snowballs, because the snow was gray and scattered with black fragments of dirt.

Soon, Maxim came out into a clearing — a green hillock covered with merry freckles of dandelions. Here the path forked. One path stretched out to the upper edge of the slope, again through the thicket, and the other went down. Maxim chose the lower path, closer to the water.

The river was fenced by a barrier of bark pieces, dry branches and other litter. Here and there lay wooden planks and even logs. Maxim recalled that it was called driftwood. Among this driftwood you could find some interesting things. Maxim kept walking along, stepping over the planks and broken branches, leaving his footprints on the narrow sandy strip.

But soon the strip ended, crossed by a brook running down the slope. Although it was small, it had dug out a whole canyon in the loose earth, and made a slush of clay and sand on the river shore.

And there was no bridge.

Maxim glanced up. No, he had no desire to squeeze his way up through the scratching jungle and then over the canyon. After that he would spend another hour picking the burrs off himself.

Maxim squinted towards the opposite side of the brook with a squinted eye. The width of the slush was about four meters, and the depth seemed very small, up to his heels.

Should he retreat from this rivulet after all the brave deeds he had done today?

He took off his sandals, pushed his socks inside and threw them over the brook. Then carefully, but without fear, he stepped into the slush.

Oh my, it was so cold! It was probably the water from the snow remains, or it was fed by cold springs. Maxim had immediately sunk up to his calves and jerked a shoulder. Pulling out his feet with a squelching sound, he reached the brook. It was even colder. Maxim sank deeper, up to his knees, and the edge of his bandage got wet. But the end of the dangerous way was at hand. Maxim made a step, then another one... and suddenly felt that he could go no further: when he tried to raise one foot, the other at once sank deeper.

At first Maxim was not afraid. He simply stopped so that he could think how to get out. But hardly had he begun thinking than he realized that he was sinking, even when he stood motionless. Deep silence surrounded him, and only above, the humming of invisible cars could be heard.

Maxim remembered the stories about quicksand, when people had disappeared into it completely, and he felt cold not only in his feet but even on the back of his head.

Could it happen to him? Was it possible? And in several days they would find his wet field cap.... Or maybe they would find nothing at all! The rain would just wash away his footsteps on the sand leading to the brook....

And what would Mama and Papa think? And Andrew?

Confound it! What rubbish was getting into his head, while he was just a meter and a half from the solid ground! After all, he could dive out flat and stretch out his hand to that dry ledge with tall weeds.

But falling down in the slush! What about his uniform?

He jerked angrily forward. But the mire didn't let him go so easily, and he had sunk down above his knees. The bandage had disappeared.

Maxim's fear grew, too. Of course, he didn't seriously think he could drown. Instead, he thought the slush would get through his bandage to the wound and then he would certainly get some infection. But he remembered he had had a jab, and of course he needn't be afraid of germs. Another danger was more serious: his legs hurt from the cold, and he could end up getting pneumonia. In any case, Maxim would become hoarse for a long time. How will he sing then? And what about the Pioneer meeting where he was going to become a Pioneer?

But those thoughts didn't last long. He was sinking. The icy slush went up his legs and almost got to his shorts. Now he couldn't reach the ground even if he fell down! Should he cry out?

Maxim desperately gazed at the overgrown slope. Who would hear him? And, apart from the situation being appalling, crying out would be humiliating.

It's another matter if you are drowning in the river. But to cry out "help!" after getting stuck on dry land because of your own foolishness?

The edges of his shorts had already touched the slush and had started getting wet. Maybe he could still lunge out flat and get out by working with his arms and legs as hard as he could?

Maxim gazed at the slope once more... and saw a girl running down from above, jumping from ledge to ledge. In her hands was a pole. Maxim realized straightaway that it was a girl, even though she had a short haircut and wore jeans with a striped T-shirt resembling a sailor's striped vest. She cried out in an agitated, girlish voice:

"Oh, steady, wait a moment, I'm coming!"

Chapter eight

CINDERELLA AND PRINCE

On the firm ground, Maxim recovered his breath and gave a sideways glance at the girl. He felt that he didn't look like a conquering hero: he was tousled, scared and had filthy legs. The recent danger now seemed a trifle. A big deal to get bogged down above the knees! The girl was probably giggling to herself over his fright. Maxim made an indifferently-annoying face and said jauntily:

"D-damn it.... Got in a real mess, indeed! A bit more and I would be as dirty as a piglet."

"It's not very dangerous here," said the girl. "You wouldn't sink above your waist."

Maxim again cast a quick glance at the girl: was it a joke? But no, there wasn't any trace of laughter in her eyes. She was just reassuring him. He shrugged his shoulders.

"Above the waist! I can imagine what I would look like then! I am pretty well covered in mud as it is!"

He looked at his legs. They looked as though he was wearing gray-spotted wet socks. Streams of slush still flowed down them, leaving light stripes. Maxim shifted from one dirty foot to the other and went to the water to wash them clean.

The girl grasped him by his sleeve.

"Don't be crazy! The water's so cold!"

Maxim's feet were still aching from cold, but he bravely smiled:

"I think it's no colder than in there," and he pointed to the brook.

"Don't go there, please. Let's go up. There's a fire hydrant over there. And your bandage needs to be changed, too."

So, she managed to make out his bandage under the layer of clay?

"And where can I get a new bandage?" asked Maxim.

"Come on."

Maxim shrugged his shoulders, as men do when giving way to a woman's whim. He picked up his sandals and followed the girl who was climbing up along a snake-like path.

Walking barefoot was not easy. Every now and then tiny sharp stones got under his feet. Maxim stumbled several times, and he almost lost his balance once because he couldn't get a grip on the plant stalks with his sandals in one hand and the boltik in the other. Even when he was grasping the pole that had saved him, he hadn't let it slip out of his hand. The faithful companion was still with Maxim. And, feeling its ribbed weight, he felt a calm joy, despite all the mishaps.

They had climbed up the high bank and found themselves in an old side street, which looked very similar to the one where Maxim had found the gold chip and the boltik. The sidewalk was pierced with burdocks, and a hydrant stood nearby. The girl made an effort and raised the starting-lever. The hydrant quacked, stirred and struck the concrete slab with its round, glassy jet. Fine droplets of water formed a mist, and several little rainbows encircled Maxim's rescuer.

"Here you are, wash your legs," she said in a commanding tone.

Maxim put his legs under the strong jet. After the cold brook, the water seemed very warm, as though it had been heated. The clay was washed off in a few seconds! Hopping now on one leg then on the other, Maxim hurriedly pulled his socks on and buckled his sandals. Then he straightened out his uniform, adjusted his field cap and became again a correct and good-looking Maxim Rybkin — almost the same as he had been when leaving home; only his bandage remained gray and dirty, and the edge of his shorts had a dark hem of damp clay.

"I guess the dirt has got under your bandage," the girl said again, "you need to change it."

"But where—" began Maxim, but she interrupted him:

"Stay here, I'll fetch one quickly. I live nearby. Don't even think of going away."

Maxim slightly smiled.

"Why should I go away?"

She smiled too, and for the first time they looked at each other's faces not furtively but directly.

"I know...," said the girl. "Boys are so fearful. They're even afraid of pulling a splinter out, let alone to be bandaged."

"Ha-ha! What next!" replied Maxim.

"So, wait here."

"Okay."

She ran away, turning around once; and he stood by the hydrant watching her running.

The girl disappeared around the corner. Maxim, limping a little (his knee had begun aching again), came up to the bench next to a nearby gate, sat down and prepared to wait.

But the girl was already coming back, again at a run. She returned so quickly that the drops of water, which had clung to her rust-colored hair from the hydrant jet, still had not dried out. In her fist she held a sterile dressing package and little nail scissors.

Maxim sighed quietly and stretched his leg. The girl squatted in front of Maxim and looked up at him. At first she was looking seriously. Then they smiled a bit again. It was as though some fine thread had stretched out between them. As if they understood something without words. It was unclear what it was, but all the same they both felt good.

The girl bent forward, clicked with her scissors and started unwinding the wet bandage. And without raising her eyes she said suddenly in a low voice:

"My name's Tanya...."

"And I'm Maxim."

The girl's fingers stopped for a second, as if she wondered at such a name or she simply wanted to remember it better. Then she quickly, but carefully, removed the bandage.

Maxim glanced at his open knee and averted his eyes: the picture was not much fun.

"Oh, gosh!" said Tanya. "How did you manage to graze it so badly?"

"Well, it was an accident... because of a woman," said Maxim, indifferently looking over Tanya's head. He was glad that he could tell of his heroism without boasting. "I was walking along the street, and she stood there shouting: 'Oh, my flat will catch fire! Oh, we'll burn down!' She had left her flat and hadn't turned her clothes iron off. In addition, the door was locked, and she hadn't taken the key with her. Everybody stood and sighed. What would happen if a fire really started? Well, then I climbed up to the third floor and turned the iron off. It really was about to catch fire — everything was in smoke there.... And when I started climbing down I fell.... And after that the woman caught up with me and said that I had pinched her money!"

Maxim remembered how it had been, and his voice faltered with resentment.

"They made me have two shots. It's nothing, of course; but I was late for school because of it. And after that she started demanding her money.... Ah, who cares! I was saving the house, not her."

"Yes, indeed, what a foolish woman she is," Tanya agreed. "Instead of thanking you she says such nasty things— Don't bend your leg, I'll bandage it now.... And what did you reply?"

"Me? I even got lost," admitted Maxim. "But the pilot who had brought me to the medical unit stood up for me. I wish you could have heard him answering her!"

"It serves her right!" answered Tanya.

She was speaking calmly, outwardly restrained, but her heart was thumping quickly and joyfully. Because she was doing what she had been dreaming of! She was bandaging the wounded, heroic prince, and not in her dream, but in earnest. Well, he didn't kill dragons or battle with enemies; he simply saved a house from fire. And not only that! He had climbed an awful height and got a wound! And not in a fairy-tale but in reality.... It didn't matter that he hadn't a sword and silky cloak. Where could you find a prince with a sword nowadays? Maxim was brave and good-looking anyway.

Of course, Tanya knew that boys are boys. Even princes. They can boast a little or do some foolish things. But nothing can be done about it. Mama had said, many times, that even adult men can be airheads. And the little ones have it even more. But fairy-tale heroes don't live in the real world. Anyway, Maxim resembled a prince more than anybody else, and Tanya had seen it at once. The main thing was, he didn't put on airs in front of a girl, not in the least.... Although, how could he put on airs being bogged down in clay up to his stomach? Then, he could have gone away, but on the contrary he said what his name was. And maybe.... Maybe he had been dreaming of his Cinderella for a long time, too?

And if he had not, maybe he was beginning to dream of her now? After all, she had saved him and dressed his wound.... She tightened the knot and straightened up.

"There you are."

Maxim stood up too.

Tanya thought, "Now he'll say 'Well, thank you, I'll go now,' and leave for good."

"Your bandage isn't too tight, is it?" asked Tanya hurriedly. "Maybe it's better to put a new dressing on it?"

Maxim carefully bent his leg.

"It's a bit tight, but it's nothing. It'll come loose and be right as rain...." And added belatedly, "Thank you."

He had said "thank you" and suddenly realized he
didn't know what to do next. Should he say, "Well, bye!"
and go to the park? It was somehow not right to leave in
this way. And, to tell the truth, he didn't even want to.

Maxim glanced at the bandage and then at Tanya.
She was looking inquiringly and a bit guiltily. Then she
got embarrassed and began shoving her scissors into a
tight knee pocket on her jeans.

"Don't," said Maxim. "If you stumble down it'll pierce
your leg."

"I won't stumble."

"Who knows," argued Maxim seriously. "I also didn't
think that I would crash down so soundly.... And then I
became bogged down in that mush. I also didn't expect
it.... It's so good that you were nearby," he added
unexpectedly, because he suddenly remembered, very
clearly, that sticky, icy slush and his helplessness. For a
moment he even forgot that he had to look brave, and
said sincerely: "I even got frightened there, a bit."

"You were taken by surprise," soothed Tanya,
"Anybody would be frightened."

Maxim thought that she was good. And it was good
that he got stuck in the brook.

"And what were you doing down there?" asked Tanya.

"I was making my way to the park."

"Along the river?" wondered Tanya.

"So what?"

"Well..., I just thought that going along the street
would be easier."

"But it's very interesting down there. It's like going
through a jungle. I've never seen such a shore, because
we lived in another town."

He noticed that Tanya was glad to hear it:

"Yes, it's really like being in a jungle, and savages
watch out for you!"

"Yes..., and you can find a secret place with hidden
treasure."

Tanya sighed shortly, glanced at Maxim uncertainly,
and, for some reason, paled a little.

"Do you know... there's a secret there. You won't give it away?"

"Not on my life," said Maxim hurriedly and felt thrilled, too.

"Then, let's go. Give me your hand— Oh, what's in your fist?"

"It's a boltik," Maxim smiled. "I'd found it this morning. It's been with me all day." He opened his hand.

"It's good. Don't lose it," said Tanya. "Well, let's go."

And they started descending along the small path.

Chapter nine

THE SWALLOW'S NEST

It was a ledge overgrown with a grassy thicket, which could be seen neither from above nor from below. It was invisible even from the path that ran three steps away. Tanya pulled Maxim by his hand; they slipped between the huge burdocks and found themselves on a narrow cornice.

"A secret ledge," thought Maxim with pleasure. And all of a sudden he saw a crack. A big layer of soil turned aside as if it had been sliced by a giant's knife. But it didn't fall down because it was joined with the slope by a network of roots, all covered with grit and cobwebs.

"Come in," said Tanya in a whisper and slipped sidelong into the crack. So Maxim went, carefully trying not to soil his uniform, which had already been messed up pretty badly. It was pitch-dark, and only green spots were floating before his eyes.

"Wait, I've got to find my secret string switch," whispered Tanya. She groped her way and soon found it, because an electric torch had turned on and lighted up the secret cave with a bright pool of light.

What was this? A pirates' den, an underground vault of a knight's castle, a wigwam, a captain's cabin? Or all of those combined?

It was a small room, perhaps even a burrow, dug into the thickness of the steep bank. The size was a bit more than a box that would hold an upright piano. The earthy ceiling nearly touched Maxim's field cap. The walls were clad with pieces of plywood, Maxim gradually made out, as he was initially dazzled by the bright glitter of silver stars. They were cut out from aluminum foil and stuck to the walls. A red plywood shield, with a coat of arms depicting a yellow winged lion, and two wooden swords hung down opposite the entrance. And on the other walls Maxim saw a crossbow, two bows, an old fencing sword, a quiver, quite a big spyglass, a map of South America and a magnificent Indian headdress.

"Have you done it all by yourself?" asked Maxim in amazement. Tanya quickly turned around. Her eyes were sparkling in the light of the torch.

"This cave was already here. I've just made it a bit deeper. And then I've done all this. Do you like it?"

"To be sure!" said Maxim.

What a girl she was!

"Did you make these weapons yourself, too?"

"Of course I did. It was last year.... Nobody knows about this cave, only me.... And now you...."

"Yes, hardly anybody will find this place," said Maxim knowingly. "The slope is steep, the entrance isn't visible.... If enemies tried to get in it's possible to hold the line one against a hundred. Cool place!"

Where the enemies could come from Maxim did not know, but he distinctly imagined them clambering up through the bushes. They were clad in animal hides, with axes and in solid helmets looking like pails with slits for eyes. And he would stand at the edge of the precipice, knocking them down the slope with a sparkling sword, defending Tanya. Although, she probably wouldn't like to be defended and would take a sword herself.

"And the approach is easily kept in sight," he continued. "May I look at your crossbow?"

"Of course!"

Tanya hurriedly took the weapon from a nail. Maxim rested the wooden stock against his stomach, pulled back and hooked the rubber bowstring. Then he took an arrow from the quiver, put it onto the groove and aimed at the light crack of the entrance through which could be seen the waving grass tops.

"Only don't shoot for nothing, the arrow will get lost," warned Tanya. And quickly changed her mind, "No, shoot if you like, of course!"

"No, I won't," said Maxim. "Indeed, it would be a pity to lose it."

He put back the arrow and ran the bowstring free.

"May I try this war bonnet on?" he pointed at the Indian headdress.

"Take it. And I'll try on your field cap, OK?"

The field cap made Tanya look like a boy. It was difficult to say what Maxim resembled in his Indian chief headdress: he couldn't see himself. Was there a mirror?

Ah yes, there was! A small mirror with a chipped corner hung in a small niche. And in the same niche, as though on the stage of a tiny theater, crowded multicolored musketry, pages and ladies-in-waiting. All made of plasticine. A box of new plasticine bars lay nearby. Maxim glanced at the sumptuous court circle with some curiosity, but decided to look at it later. The decoration on his head interested him more. Scratching his plumage against the clay ceiling he took up a warlike position in front of the mirror.

Of course, his snub nose and fair eyebrows did not look like the aquiline face of an Iroquois chief. The feathers also had been taken not from an eagle, but most likely from a hen, and then painted in different colors. But all the same, Maxim felt that an Indian warrior looked very similar. And he said to Tanya in a happy whisper:

"Cool! The terror of all western prairies!"

She appeared at his side in the field cap. Their heads were side by side, and Tanya's hair was tickling Maxim's cheek. The old mirror showed two smiling faces.

"I look like a stewardess, don't I?" said Tanya.

"Why a stewardess?" Maxim resented the suggestion slightly, "you look just like a pilot."

"Tell me about this field cap," she asked. "And in general, what sort of clothes are you wearing? It's some uniform, isn't it?"

"Of course it's a uniform," he said.

And at that moment he couldn't help but pull Tanya's leg. As if somebody made him say it! Yes, it happens sometimes: one moment you have absolutely no wish to tell lies, then suddenly deceitful words leap out from you, all by themselves!

"This is the uniform of the school for young cosmonauts," he said in a most usual tone of voice.

And at once he got scared! What if Tanya watched television that morning and understood what a bragger he was? But no, if she had done she wouldn't have asked him about it now. She looked surprised but, at the same time, spoke with respect.

"What? The school for young cosmonauts? Is it a sort of hobby group?"

It was an opportunity to say "I was joking," but she was looking in such a way that Maxim couldn't stop:

"Not a group. It's a school. Grown-up cosmonauts are trained in a preparation center, and we, schoolchildren, in a preparation school."

Tanya sat down on a wooden box and took Maxim by his hand.

"Sit down. Tell me."

Maxim sighed and sat down next to her. His conscience had already been tormenting him as a dentist's drill would do, but his tongue was living a life of its own. There was nowhere to retreat now.

"This school prepares children for future space missions," said Maxim with the most serious air. "It's only now children are not allowed into space, but soon they'll fly too. When we inhabit other planets. It'll be very soon. That's why they opened this school. It's not a well-known school. It's not a secret place, but nevertheless.... It is linked with cosmonautics."

Now Tanya was looking at him distrustfully, half smiling. And after being silent for a while she said condescendingly:

"Cosmonauts don't wear short trousers."

This caused him confusion and resentment. Maxim wanted to say "Believe it or not!" but changed his mind. It would sound as though he couldn't prove his words. But now he almost believed in his space school himself. And he said calmly and convincingly:

"But we're not grown-ups yet. We're the youngest group, and we're only training. But anyway, some day we're to fly into outer space."

"What about a Pioneer's word of honor?" asked Tanya. She said it not in a demanding voice, but rather pitifully.

Maxim sadly shook his head.

"You see, I'm not a Pioneer yet. Do you know when we'll be admitted? Only after—" He stopped short of saying "after the first flight." It would be just a barefaced lie. And he said: "after a training course. I'm still to take two tests on weightlessness...."

Tanya kept staring at him, not at his face, but a bit lower. It seemed she was looking at his red star badge.

"Now she'll say, 'Give me the Oktyabryata's word of honor' — and that will be the end," thought Maxim.

She didn't say it. She took off the field cap and began examining its silver wings.

"Maybe he isn't bragging," Tanya thought. "Maybe indeed, there is such a school.... But if he is bragging — so what? He is a boy after all. It's excusable. Anyway, he's brave and handsome. He just doesn't understand it and wants to look better. Well, it's nothing. But instead, he understood at once what a good place her cave was. And he knew about weapons, just as a real prince would, wearing his sword all his life...."

"Do you know what I call this cave? 'The Swallow's Nest,'" she said.

"Because it's on a steep slope," responded Maxim knowingly. "They always build their nests in such places."

"So, do you like it here?"

"Yes, of course I do," said Maxim sincerely.

"Only don't tell anybody."

"No, I won't. I've already promised."

"And you... you can come here whenever you like, even without me...."

"All right," said Maxim in a low voice. "But... it would be better with you."

And suddenly he realized completely what a swine and bragger he was when telling tales about the space school. How could he speak and laugh now with an open heart? Besides, she would learn the truth anyway. Then would it be possible to come into "The Swallow's Nest?"

He felt so angry that he involuntarily struck his knee with his fist holding the boltik. The bandaged knee. The pain throbbed all over his body. Maxim clenched his teeth, took off the Indian headdress and hung it up on the nail. Then he closed his eyes tight, and with his eyes still closed, softly said:

"Tanya, I lied to you... about the space school."

He cast a quick glance at her.

Tanya, it seemed, was not surprised. And most important of all, she didn't take offence. There was even a kind of gladness in her eyes. She just asked:

"And what's your uniform, then?"

"Ah, it's nothing," said Maxim with relief. "It's just a musical ensemble in the Palace of Culture. The chorus 'The Little Wings.' Today we've appeared on television."

"Really?!"

Maxim was surprised: what did he say that was so special?

He did not understand her because Tanya was a girl. And girls love famous singers almost as much as cosmonauts.

Of course, not every boy singing in a chorus is a famous singer, but if he had appeared on television....

At first she was happy, but then knitted her brows with distrust.

"And what if you... well, just imagined it again?"

"No, I am not!" said Maxim, hastily touching his star badge. "Word of honor! And you can ask anybody if we were on television this morning! I sang a song about pilots. Don't you believe me?"

Now he didn't think of boasting at all. He just wanted her to believe him, as hard as he could. If the story appeared a bit boastful it was completely by chance!

Tanya believed him. And once again she said:

"Sit down. Tell me."

"But don't be angry."

"What for?"

"Well..., for my monkey business."

"But you told me at once that you were joking— Is it frightening to sing on stage?"

"No. That is, it is a bit, while you're waiting to sing. And when you're singing you don't feel afraid any more.... Besides, this boltik is helping me today," Maxim smiled and opened his palm again. "I was singing with it."

Tanya nodded seriously and rolled the boltik on Maxim's palm with her finger.

"Yes, it must be easy with it.... Was the song good?"

"And how!"

"Can you sing it now?"

"Now?"

"So what? Please sing it," Tanya requested. "Don't be shy, forget I am sitting here. Sing as if you are alone."

But Maxim of course felt shy. And asked rather stupidly:

"What for?"

"Well...," she said calmly. "I didn't watch the concert, but I'd like to. It would be lovely to hear your song...."

"There's no acoustics here."

"There's no what?"

"It's a very small place so the sound won't be good. And there's no music or chorus, either. This song's for choral singing."

"But try and sing it yourself. Maybe you'll manage it! I'll understand. First sing as a chorus and then as yourself."

She spoke pleadingly and at same time rather insistently, looking right into his eyes. And all of a sudden Maxim realized that he might be looking like a storyteller again: he had talked a lot about the concert, but was refusing to sing. Tanya might think he was telling a lie and really take offence. But that was not the only thing.

The thing was, that Maxim wanted to sing. He felt confused, but wanted to anyway.... So, suppressing his embarrassment, he said in a faltering voice:

"All right. Only I don't know.... It'll be as it will be."

"Yes, of course!" Tanya said hastily. She sprang to her feet and drew back to the wall.

Maxim took a long breath, unfolded his shoulders, set his fists against the box. Then he looked at the sunny clouds in the bright slit of the entrance. They were pierced by the white thread from a jet plane.

Maxim started singing:

> *"The sun has just arisen*
> *A breeze has touched the grass.*
> *The town's little airfield has awoken all at once..."*

To tell the truth, he was singing instead of the chorus, without full effort, because it was just an introduction. When the chorus words ended, Maxim paused, mentally counting musical beats. And started to sing his part without timidity, clearly and with expression:

> *"Comrade pilot!*
> *For you, it's so easy!..."*

And his desperate wish for the flight, the hope for a miracle and yearning for the sky's height had come to Maxim again.

> *"I want for a minute to fly over fields*
> *I often dream of it in the night*
> *Take me, I'm very light!"*

And of course, in the end he had been taken on. And he solemnly told about it in the song. After he finished singing, he sat motionless for some time, as if returning from the flight to this place, to "The Swallow's Nest." He looked inquiringly at Tanya.

"Atta boy!" she said. "It's great, honest! Will you invite me to a concert, next time?"

He nodded. There were many concerts ahead, and of course he'd invite her. And Mama and Papa too, and probably even his sarcastic brother, and the girls and boys from his class....

Having thought of his class Maxim became anxious.

"Do you know, it's time for me to go," he said in a downcast tone of voice. "My class is there, and I ought be there, too. Or they'll scold me."

"That's a pity," said Tanya confusedly lowering her

eyes.

Maxim didn't want to go, either. He felt sorry at the thought that maybe they would never have such a good meeting again. And although Tanya had said, "Come when you wish," who knew what could happen....

"You know.... Let's go to the park together," he said, even surprising himself.

"Me?"

"Uh-huh. Let's go!"

"But... your class... I don't know any of them."

"So what? You are with me," said Maxim gamely.

Chapter ten

THE FIGHT

The town where Maxim had previously lived was built recently. And the trees in that town were young, too. They were thin and did not hide the sun at all. But this was an old park, with branchy poplars and maples. And though their leaves were still small, the trees gave good shade anyway. The branches had got entangled and made up a green canopy.

Maxim and Tanya entered the park. The green air was pierced by thin sunbeams, and they covered the sandy paths with round dots resembling yellow confetti. Maxim stepped on them thoughtfully, and they were dancing on his legs; those sunlight spots seemed warm and quite fluffy.

A few visitors were walking along the main pathway, but no children were in sight, neither Maxim's classmates nor any others. But soon, from afar, they began to hear a many-voiced merry noise. It was probably the place where children from Maxim's class were enjoying themselves. But Maxim didn't feel like hurrying up and running. It was good just to walk slowly under the green covering of poplars and maples. And so they were walking, holding each other's hands.

Then Maxim saw Svetka Meshalkina from his class, who was coming out of the park.

Meshalkina had noticed him as well and stopped.

"Coo! Rybkin.... What a smart uniform!"

But she looked at Maxim just briefly because she was staring at Tanya.

"Rybkin, where've you been? We thought you'd fallen ill."

"'Fallen ill!'" thought Maxim. "Didn't they watch the concert?"

"You thought right," he said angrily. "I was in hospital, in fact. Got two shots against blood poisoning."

But talking about the shots didn't impress her. She continued to look at Tanya with curiosity.

"Where are our folk?" asked Maxim.

"Where.... In the amusement pavilions, of course. Over there," she waved her hand back.

"And where are you going?"

"I asked to leave. Anyway I don't like these crazy merry-go-rounds, but I've got a lot to do at home. Besides, I have to prepare my Pioneer uniform for the day after tomorrow meeting. Have you prepared yours?"

"Yes, I have," replied Maxim trying to sound nonchalant, but feeling inside a ping of joy when he thought of the big forthcoming day.

"Look out! I bet Rimma Vasilievna will ask you about it as soon as she sees you."

"Oh, she's here?"

"Yes, she is. You don't know anything. Sofia Ivanovna was called to a conference, and Rimma Vasilievna came with us to see what kind of troop we are."

"I bet she's said that we aren't well disciplined," guessed Maxim.

"Of course! Tylikov's letting us down, as usual. He behaves like... I don't even know who. Like Tylikov, in short."

"Well, we'll go. Bye," said Maxim and went with Tanya towards the amusement pavilions, indicated by a blue signpost.

Svetka, of course, stood still staring after them. Then she called Maxim:

"Rybkin! Wait a moment!"

Maxim unwillingly stopped and approached her.

"What?"

"Who's that?" asked Meshalkina in a whisper and gave Tanya a quick glance.

Maxim restrained himself and said with a challenge:

"It's Tanya, an acquaintance of mine, what do you care?"

"I don't care at all," said Svetka in an indifferent tone of voice and started looking at the bushy treetops. "But they'll laugh. They'll say that you've brought your fiancée."

"What a fool!" flared up Maxim.

"No, I am not. You saw I didn't laugh," said Svetka calmly. "Well, bye, Rybkin. I'm off."

"Get lost!"

He turned back to Tanya, took her hand and tightly pressed the boltik in the other. And they headed for the forthcoming merry clutter.

The avenue of trees ended and Maxim could see the amusement pavilions. Here and there multicolored swing boats flew up and down. The whirling merry-go-rounds looked like fancy colored umprellas with little horses and planes attached to them. The wheel from the giant's bicycle was slowly rotating in the sky, lifting up the passenger cabins to an awesome height. They almost brushed against the sunny clouds. From earth, their passengers looked like multicolored Lilliputians. And they probably felt great, up there in the sky. As if they were flying....

Maxim wanted to get there so much that his heart began aching.

But first he ought to explain himself to Rimma Vasilievna. Where was she? What a bustle! It seemed that excursions had been organized in many of the town's schools today. Boys and girls were rushing about in all directions, queuing up for merry-go-rounds, playing leapfrog, swarming around soda selling machines. On one lawn, first graders were singing and dancing in a ring, supervised by two big girls, and on another, a whole class surrounded their teacher and they were rehearsing something, quite noisily.

Among this hustle and bustle Maxim caught sight of a red field cap.

Rimma Vasilievna had become the Chief Pioneer Leader long ago, and she had a habit of wearing a red field cap with a little tassel on the front. She liked it so much that she wore it in school, out of school and, perhaps, even at home. It looked as though she was born with it. Her little light-yellow ringlets curled out from under the field cap in quite a girlish way. And furthermore, when she wore her white blouse, she looked like an eighth grader. But only from a distance. When you came closer you could see that she was already an adult, not just because of her wrinkles — there were hardly any, maybe some crow's feet — it seemed to Maxim that her lips looked like the lips of a very old lady, although made-up. She probably knew it and kept them pursed, making her mouth resemble a thin chink. It gave her a resolute air.

"Wait," said Maxim to Tanya. He approached Rimma Vasilievna and said hello to her.

"Ah, here you are!" she said. "They told me you were ill. Why didn't you come to school at one thirty, as everybody else did?"

"I was in hospital, because of my leg."

Rimma Vasilievna glanced at his bandage.

"Well, tell that to your headmistress when she returns. And now join the other children and do what everybody else is doing. Then, when I give a call, come to me at once."

"Where is my class and what are they doing?" asked Maxim.

"They are having a good time in the amusement pavilions," she said, then added with unexpected annoyance, "although somebody, like Tylikov, is running all over the place, undermining discipline. I don't recommend that you follow his example if you are going to become a Pioneer the day after tomorrow. Behave yourself. Understood?"

"Yes, I will," said Maxim softly.

"By the way, I hope your Pioneer uniform is ready. Is

it?"

"Yes, it is. It has been for a long time."

"Well, you can go then."

Maxim ran up to Tanya:

"Let's go to the Ferris wheel!"

"No, it's so high. I'll die up there!"

"No, you won't," Maxim reassured her. And out of the blue he promised: "I'll hold your hand, doubly tight."

At once he got confused and kicked an empty ice-cream cup. Tanya quickly nodded and lowered her eyes.

They went up to the wheel pavilion. Oh, what good luck! Almost all Maxim's class had gathered here. There was even Tylikov, who calmly stood in the queue behind Vera Kovalchuk. He saw Maxim first and said loudly:

"Hurray! Fresh forces for parachute troops!"

Everybody turned around: "Hi, Max! Where did you come from? They said you'd been unwell today!" Mishka Stremenko asked mockingly, "What's that red uniform on you? Have you enrolled in the fire-brigade?"

What a goose! Didn't he watch television?

And in general it was strange: nobody said a word about the concert. They didn't even nickname him a yodeler star. Just as though there had never been a concert! Could it be that they all missed the concert because of it being the first day of summer?

Maxim cast perplexed glances at his classmates.

Nobody, except Mishka, paid any attention to his suit. Though it could be because of the very warm weather — everybody had left their school uniforms at home, and Maxim did not stand out in this motley crowd. But why did the children say nothing about the concert?

Oh yes, it was clear, nobody had watched it! They had probably read the word "concert," and that was enough not to turn the TV on. What people! Certainly they were always ready to watch cartoons.... It seems he was too modest when he didn't tell them about today's concert.

Maxim even forgot about Tanya for a moment because of those thoughts. But he quickly came to his senses, and they joined the queue.

The enormous wheel was rotating above them carrying away the cabins with those lucky people who had waited their turn.

Maxim threw back his head, and his heart missed a beat from happy expectation. Soon he would be up there, too.... He didn't notice that many were watching him and Tanya. The girls were whispering. Mishka Stremenko was telling Vera Kovalchuk something. Vera loudly answered that he was a blockhead.

Tanya pulled her hand out of Maxim's fingers.

"Stay here, OK? I'll drop in to the bookstall. They're selling stamps there, and I'm collecting stamps about the cosmos."

"Only don't be long," replied Maxim.

Vera Kovalchuk glanced at Maxim and suddenly said:

"I don't want to go on the wheel. I'd rather go to the swings. It's too long to wait here."

"I know, you're afraid," said Tylikov impishly.

"So what if I am? Not everyone's a hero like you."

"Fewer people, more oxygen," grinned Stremenko.

"Fewer? There is nothing in it for you! I'll put Rybkin in my place. Come on, Maxim."

That was great! He had overtaken ten people in one go.

"Yeah, the girls love Rybkin. For them he's like honey for the bees," Stremenko avenged himself.

Maxim said nothing: fools cannot be cured with words.

"And who was that girl with you?" asked Tylikov all of a sudden. This time he asked in a good way, simply and not mockingly. And Maxim answered in the same way:

"She's an acquaintance of mine, Tanya. Imagine, today I got stuck on the shore in clay and she dragged me out. I was sinking in there like in a bog. Gosh! If she hadn't been in time, I'd have been covered in filth from top to toe."

"I wondered why you have clay on your clothes," noted Tylikov sympathetically and with his finger he picked at a dried gray stripe on Maximka's shorts.

"Oh, never mind! It'll peel off itself," said Maxim.

"And what about your concert? Was it OK?" asked Tylikov unexpectedly, in a low voice.

Maxim's heart fluttered.

"Yes..., everything was fine.... Did you watch it?"

"Nope, my mother sent me to the grocery and then to the drugstore."

"But how do you know about the concert, then?"

Tylikov grinned, wanted to say something, but Tanya returned at that moment so he said nothing.

"Oh, the queue has moved so fast," said Tanya cheerfully.

"Stand with me," said Maxim, nudging Tylikov with his shoulder.

Mishka Stremenko retorted:

"Just look at him! 'Stand with me!' She wasn't in the queue, was she?"

"But we are together," said Maxim.

"You were, when you stood further back. But Verka only gave her place to you!"

"We want to go on the ride together."

"She isn't from our class!"

"So what? Isn't she a human after all?"

"Why are you picking on them!" said Tylikov. "Let them stay."

"Tylikov, mind your own business! They ought to queue up like everyone else!"

"Well, Tanya, let's go to the old place," said Maxim proudly. The old place was behind Vladik Polyakovsky, a short and calm boy, but now that lanky, bad tempered Zinka Stupicina was standing behind him.

"We were standing here," declared Maxim to Zinka. "Vladik, tell her."

"Yeah, they were," Vladik confirmed willingly.

"I don't care about that," said Zinka in a scandalous tone. "Those who stood here are standing here now, and if someone left his place he has only himself to blame."

"We were standing here," said Maxim emphatically and tried to push Zinka aside with his elbow. But Zinka was a head taller than him and she pushed Maxim off herself, quite resolutely.

"A walking fire tower!" said Maxim in temper. Certainly, he couldn't fight with her. It would be ridiculous and nothing good would come out of it: she could thrash him, despite the fact she was a girl. But retreating was not an option, either. "I'm telling you, let me in!"

"What a cry I hear!"

The voice was familiar and mocking. Maxim even started: behind him was Vitka Transistor!

Transya didn't look like himself. He was tidy, in new jeans and a white shirt. And pinned on his shirtsleeve was an armband with big letters "OP." Maxim guessed at once it was "Order Patrol", which Rimma Vasilievna had recently spoken about.

But why was Transya, who had given no peace to anybody, taken into the patrol? Maybe he had changed and started to behave himself? No, it was unlikely. He did have a polished air about him, but his eyes were still nasty. Behind him stood two unknown boys, probably fifth or six graders.

"What a cry? Let's have some order, here!" repeated Transya with a caustic smile. "Is Rybkin behaving badly? Aye-aye, what an ill-mannered boy...."

"I was standing here!" said Maxim.

"He was," confirmed Vladik and earned a clip on the back of his head from Zinka.

"He doesn't know himself where he's standing," said Mishka Stremenko (why, had Maxim done him any harm?). "First he's standing here, and now there. And she wasn't standing here at all," said Mishka pointing his finger at Tanya.

"You weren't standing here yourself," said Tylikov.

"They were! We saw them!" said the girls that were ahead.

"What's going on here?" said a grown-up voice suddenly and at once everyone became quiet. It was Roza Mikhailovna, the 3B class-mistress. She was an elderly, strict looking woman, with a black hairstyle resembling a Caucasian woolen hat. "Why such a mess? Is Tylikov running the show again?"

"Whatever happens I am always first to be picked on," said Tylikov.

"It's Rybkin," explained Transya knowingly. "It's well-behaved, quiet Rybkin getting out of turn, and in addition with his girlfriend."

"We were standing here!" cried Maxim.

"Keep quiet," said Roza Mikhailovna. "Everybody should stand in their own places. Get in line." And she took herself off, fully confident that she had put the place in order and settled the dispute.

"So, is that all clear to you small fry?" asked Transya. "Line up! And the end is o-o-ver there! Off you go...." And he pointed to the end of the queue, which had just been joined by another class, with its full complement.

"Maxim, let's go somewhere else," said Tanya in a whisper. "Don't bother with him."

Maxim still wanted to take a ride on the Ferris wheel, but it was sickening to stand here after what had happened.

"Let's go to the shooting gallery. I can spend fifty kopecks instead of my lunch."

And they went off, without looking back. Everybody was silent. Then Tylikov called to them:

"Max, stand in my place, and she can stand in Verka's!"

"Thanks. We're going to the shooting gallery."

They didn't know where the shooting gallery was and had got a bit lost in the park paths. Both kept silence. Maxim felt ill at ease, because of his classmates. And because of himself, too: he couldn't obtain justice. To muffle his awkwardness he said with annoyance:

"That Transya's such a troublemaker. Everybody knows it, but he's got in the patrol anyway."

"He's nasty," agreed Tanya.

An overgrown path had led them once again to the edge of the pavilion area.

And there, as if he was called, Transistor appeared again! He darted out from the bushes. Now he was alone. He looked at Maxim and Tanya and smirked gloatingly.

"Ha, ha, is a small fry swimming away? Wanted to take a ride, but didn't manage it! You see now how it's bad getting out of turn."

"Do you know what his band means?" Maxim asked Tanya loudly."'OP' — 'Offensive Pampers.'"

He was sure that Transya would not dare to touch

him while the teachers and Pioneer leaders were nearby. But he suddenly ran up to Maxim, pushed him into the bushes and rushed in next. Around there were only green branches. Transya dexterously wrenched Maxim's arm.

"Free my arm this minute!"

"Say: 'Vitenka, forgive me, I won't do it any more.'"

Maxim saw Tanya's round eyes. No, he'd rather lose his conscience than say such words.

But the pain was unbearable. Transya pressed harder, and Maxim fell down with his knees on the grass.

"Hands off, scum," he said through tears, setting his forehead against the bush root. His fingers unclenched and the boltik slipped out.

In the corner of his eye he saw Tanya had rushed with raised fists and was thrown off backward into the branchy thicket: Transya pushed her aside with his shoulder.

Then he relaxed his grip and picked Maxim up by the collar. The boltik lay on the grass. Maxim at once bent down, but Transya put his foot on it, pushed Maxim away and took the boltik himself.

"Give it back!" said Maxim.

"Oh, what a bad boy! Why do you carry it with you? Is it for fighting?"

"You're a lousy hooligan, give it back this minute!" fearlessly said Tanya.

But Transya sniggered, left the bushes and, out in the open, started making faces and teasing them with the boltik.

Tanya cast an angry eye at Maxim.

"Let's run down and thrash him!"

"How could we?" said Maxim helplessly. "We'll get into hot water ourselves. They'll say we're fighting with the Order Patrol."

Tanya said nothing and turned away. And Maxim realized that she had discovered his fear. He started rubbing his hand: Transya had almost wrenched his arm out of the shoulder joint.

"Let's go then...," Tanya said in a low voice. And off they went; Maxim kept rubbing his hand, although it almost did not hurt.

"I ought to be at home," Tanya suddenly said. "I'm

going."

Maxim stopped, perplexed.

"But what about the shooting gallery?"

"No, they'll be worrying about me at home, if I'm out too long...."

"Let's go together."

"You can't leave. You'll be scolded."

It was true.

And Maxim didn't know what to do.

"Well, I am off. Bye," said Tanya.

"Bye...," said Maxim miserably.

She turned around and slowly went off, without looking back, her head hung. And soon she disappeared behind a green pavilion where the Fun House was.

The multicolored merry-go-rounds kept whirling. Noise and laughter were heard from all sides as before. But the sun was not as bright as previously. It was as though Maxim had lost something very good or cheated somebody. Well, it was true. He'd told a lie and lost the good he had.

The sensation of loss tormented him hard also because of the boltik. Maxim was so used to it, during the day, that he even didn't think of it. It always was in his fist. But now, his hand didn't feel the habitual weight. He had lost it....

Maxim was wandering along a side alley. He didn't want to see anybody. He couldn't go far either because he could miss the assembly signal. He kept going and thought constantly how Tanya had left — she was very sad, with her head hung. It was because of him.... And if he met her again, what would he say to her? She didn't even remind him to come tomorrow....

And Transya, as if on purpose, appeared on Maxim's way again! This time he was not alone. There were three of them. They were at some distance from the alley, on a sandy patch. They knelt down and examined something on the ground. Their heads were drawn together, and they were pushing one another with their shoulders and elbows.

Next to them was a first grader in a blue sailing suit.

And he was repeating with tears:

"Give it back! Give back!"

Maxim felt so bitterly about what was going on that he almost was not afraid. Let Transya pester him again, if he wished. It didn't matter. He came up very close and saw that Transya with his pals were driving a black horned beetle to and fro. The boys pushed it with twigs, and Transya used Maxim's boltik.

"Give back...," hopelessly repeated the first grader and glanced at Maxim. From the tears his brown eyes seemed to be behind little pieces of glass.

Transya and his pals did not see Maxim. They had their backs to him and only saw the beetle.

"The beetle isn't yours!" said the first grader.

"And not yours either. It lives in the state's park, and that means it's a public beetle. And you've caught it and tormented it."

"It's you who're tormenting it! I want to take it home, and it'll live with me!"

"So, you're a poacher," said Transya and giggled. Then he gave the stag beetle such a flick that the poor thing was thrown a half meter.

Maxim glanced at the first grader's eyes again, then at Transya. He saw his back with shoulder blades moving under his shirt and tight jeans with a hip pocket. On the pocket there was a label showing a football.

Transya took aim and raised the boltik over the beetle, as though it was a seal which he wanted to stamp with all his might.

It was as if a fuse had blown up inside Maxim. Terrified at what he was about to do, he swung back his foot and gave the pocket a hearty kick with his sandal.

Transya hiccupped and buried his head in the sand. Maxim jumped on his back and started hammering Transya's neck with his fists! For himself, for Tanya, for the beetle, for the little first grader! For the boltik! For his fear and his tears!

It lasted just a second. Then everything flipped, turned over and Maxim found himself pressed to the sand. His shoulder became numb from a hard blow, and Transya had clasped him and was feeding him with sand.... And he smirked.

But he clasped him from one side, and Maxim's legs were free. Maxim desperately jerked up his right leg and struck the enemy's nose with his knee.

His knee was hard, but the nose was soft. Transya gave a squeak. Maxim managed to strike once more. And this time he hit Transya's cheekbone. Maxim felt warm, heavy drops of blood falling on his knee. Transya rolled aside.

Maxim leapt to his feet. The first thing he saw was the beetle and the boltik. The beetle was alive: it lay on its back jerking its legs. The first grader had grasped it and ran away down the alley.

And Maxim had picked up the boltik and prepared to fight tooth and nail against enraged Transya.

But he was slowly rising on to his feet. Two trickles of blood were running out of his nose, and his cheek was blue.

"What's that?"

Rimma Vasilievna was hurrying along the alley.

"Who's that?"

"It's him," groaned Transistor, smearing the blood over his cheeks: "He's a loony! Went for me as a crazy...."

"Well, well!" said Rimma Vasilievna. "Rybkin!"

"What?" said Maxim defiantly, spitting with sand. He took a tuft of grass, and wiped off Transya's red drops from his knee. Then he straightened up and put on his field cap. He was a victor. He had defended everything: "The Swallow's Nest", the boltik and himself. Transya was a skunk and everybody knew it. And the first-grader in the sailor suit would back him up.

"Was it you who started the fight?" asked Rimma Vasilievna with an icy voice.

"It was me!" said Maxim, "Because of him! He's in the patrol, but he bullies everyone!"

"When did I?" cried Transya furiously.

"No, he didn't," said his pals all together, coming at last to their senses.

Other children were coming running attracted by the noise. Roza Mikhailovna appeared.

"I'd never have thought that Rybkin was such a nasty

rough-neck," said Rimma Vasilievna. And she ordered Transya's pals, "See Vitya to the washing-stand; he must clean himself up."

Transya went off sniffing with his nose. But after two steps he turned back.

"He fought with a piece of iron! Look in his hand!"

"It's a lie!" cried Maxim.

Rimma Vasilievna unclenched his fist with her firm fingers and took the boltik.

"So, that's how it is, Rybkin...."

"But he's lying! He took it off me himself!" said Maxim desperately.

"Why are you shouting at me? It's simply a disgrace! What did he take off you? You've beaten a member of the Order Patrol till he bled!"

"But it's not true!"

"What isn't true? Well, we'll look into it at school."

Roza Mikhailovna took the Pioneer leader's hand:

"You do know that Transin is not peaches and cream...."

"Well, well, we'll get to the bottom of this."

They went a few steps aside, but Maxim heard the leader say:

"I've made such an effort to involve Transin in public affairs, but if now...."

Maxim's classmates had gathered around him.

"Now he'll give you no peace at all," said Mishka Stremenko.

Vera Kovalchuk brushed the sand off Maxim's back.

Tylikov thought and promised:

"I'll have a word with my brother. If Transya picks on you once more, he'll give him a good thrashing."

"I've got a brother of my own," said Maxim. "And I can hit back myself, if it's face to face. He thinks too much of himself...."

Rimma Vasilievna came out to the middle of the path and called, clapping her hands:

"Come here, everybody! Everybody come to me! We're going back!" Her clapping was as loud as a popgun shooting. A yellow handbag was hanging on her elbow. Maxim's boltik was in there.

Chapter eleven

THE FIGHT. PART TWO.

The bus had stopped near the school, and the third graders poured out onto the pavement. Rimma Vasilievna called for the children to gather around her.

"Nobody enters the school! The lessons are still going on; no need to make a noise there. So, everybody can go home. Remember that the day after tomorrow we are holding a Pioneer meeting. Be prepared, especially those who are going to be admitted! Bear in mind: anyone without white socks and a blue field cap may not appear at the meeting at all. Everybody dismissed! Rybkin, follow me!"

Maxim's heart ached. The Pioneer meeting would be the day after tomorrow. Everything had been ready. His ironed red tie was hanging on a clothes-hanger, to prevent it from creasing up. And, it seemed, it was all for nothing.

Rimma Vasilievna was marching along the silent school corridors; Maxim dejectedly followed her. They entered the Pioneer room. The room was flooded with sunlight. The sunbeams reflected from the yellow-varnished table, sparkled on the signal trumpets and drum hoops. The sharp tip of the banner flagpole was burning with a hot spark. The banner itself and the small class' flags were glowing with the color of fire. It was a real feast of sun and fire!

But that feast was not for Maximka. He stood in the doorway looking wistfully around the room.

Rimma Vasilievna took one of the plastic stools, sat down at the shining table, her back to the window, and put her handbag in front of her.

"Why are you standing in the doorway? Come nearer."

Maxim took several steps.

"Don't turn aside — look into my eyes when I'm speaking to you."

Feeling close to tears, Maxim raised his eyes. He forced himself. But he couldn't see Rimma Vasilievna's eyes, because she sat silhouetted against the sunlight beaming through the window. You could only see her head with curls and a pointed field cap. And her small ears shone dark red.

"I'm waiting!" said Rimma Vasilievna.

"What?" said Maxim in a husky voice.

"Oh, do I have to spell it out to you? Don't you know? I've already been waiting for a whole five minutes for you to agree to explain your wild trick."

"He started first, word of honor," said Maxim to the curls and transparent ears.

"Don't tell lies! Everybody saw how you swooped upon him, like a rooster! From behind!"

"He has also attacked me from behind, a hundred times. You didn't see from the beginning. Ask the others."

"Don't teach me what to do! I know whom and how to ask, and now I am asking you. Don't hide behind the—"

At this moment someone knocked on the door, and a teacher entered the room.

Maxim knew that it was a physics teacher, although he did not know his name. From Andrew he had heard that he was a good teacher and a cheerful, just man. Andrew called him just "Physicist."

Physicist was young, stout and fair-haired. It occurred to Maxim that he might have served in the Navy, because a weatherproof jacket with a sailor's striped top would suit him better than a teacher's gray suit and tie. However, Physicist's manner was not that of a seaman. Quite the opposite, he was upright, light and quick. His face was broad, thick-lipped and he never looked strict.

The teacher stepped further into the room, approached the table and put on it a large, smooth, metallic plate.

"Good day, dear Rimma Vasilievna."

"What's this?" wondered Rimma Vasilievna, being reflected in the plate as in a mirror.

"It's from a photo glazer." said Physicist insinuatingly. "Just look at what your 'photographers' from the Nature Friends group have done, the ones I had allowed into the photographic laboratory at your request."

"And what have they done?" asked Rimma Vasilievna crossly.

"They damaged the surface. Tell me, how it is possible to make ferrotype photos now that the glazer plate is scratched and dented? Besides that, they have broken the magnifier lamp and dropped the spare object-glass into the fixing solution."

"Where did they drop it?"

"Into the solution of hyposulphite. Or, speaking simply, into the fixing agent."

"Can we discuss it later? I ought now to finish a matter with this boy."

"Yes, I'll wait," said Physicist. He went over to a side window and started to look out. Then he unexpectedly turned around and looked closely at Maxim.

"Oh, and who's this youth in such splendid uniform? Do Pioneers dress up like this, now?"

"I don't know where he found this uniform, but this fine youth has caused an outrageous scuffle with the Patrol Order commander."

"Do you say so?" mocked Physicist. And it seemed he didn't believe her words. "Although, to look at him, I'd say that he looks like quite a well-mannered child, well, maybe a bit of a crumpled one."

"This 'well-mannered child,' for your information, has just beaten up a fifth grader with an iron screw," she said and took the boltik out of her bag.

"I didn't beat him with this screw," said Maxim in a low voice, feeling emptiness and despair inside because it was impossible to prove anything. But anyway he tried once more:

"I didn't beat him with it. He had the screw. He'd taken it off me."

"Quite right! And why had he done so?"

"Ask him, not me!" said Maxim so desperately that it sounded like a low cry.

"Why don't you behave yourself!" said Rimma Vasilievna in a threatening tone of voice. "What is going on?" And she suddenly cried at the top of her voice: "How dare you to speak to me in this way!"

Maxim gave a start and, more from fright than from desire to argue, loudly replied:

"But why are you blaming me? You said you would investigate, but you are only shouting at me."

"Oh! Just look at him...," wondered Rimma Vasilievna. "You're a tough nut, I see...."

She turned to Physicist:

"Do you see? We say 'difficult children, difficult children'... But the most difficult ones aren't those who smoke in the toilets or play truant, but like these. To look at, they're good and well bred. But they already have glib tongues to argue with adults! They debate! And he's going to be a Pioneer!"

"But, maybe first we ought to—" started Physicist, but the Pioneer leader said hurriedly:

"Well, well. Now I shall clear up the question with this fellow, and then we'll talk."

"Well, OK," agreed Physicist and started looking through the window again.

Rimma Vasilievna turned to Maxim:

"Tell me, why did you start the fight," she said, emphasizing every word.

But answering it was not an easy task: the tears were flickering in the corners of his eyes and made his voice husky. Maxim whispered:

"Because he always keeps picking on me. And he'd taken away my boltik."

"Why didn't you tell your teacher or me? You rushed to beat your comrade black and blue because of a mingy boltik!"

How could he explain? Because of the boltik? How? To tell about Tanya, of the way she had left the park? About his fight with fear, about his despair? How?!

"I just lost all patience...," said Maxim with effort.

"Whaaat?" drawled Rimma Vasilievna, and her breath became fast. "Ah, patience.... And what about me? Is my patience made of iron to put up with your daily tricks? Is it? Answer me!"

And she struck her hand on the lacquered table surface with all her might.

The plate jumped up and tinkled.

And this metallic sound evoked memories of the today's concert. It was the sound of clashed cymbals.... Dzenn! And a little fair forelock of the little musician stood on end. Dzenn! The floodlights gleamed dazzlingly in the copper plates. The trumpets were leading the resilient, vigorous melody of the march. It was a bit sad, but strong and daring at the same time.

And this melody started sounding softly inside Maxim. And, listening to it, he began straightening up.

Well, he had been holding himself upright before too, but now his head was higher, shoulders unbent; he stopped his nervous fingering of the creases on his shorts and lowered his hands. And the main thing, he had straightened in his soul. As though behind him there was a small, but brave and united orchestra. And the tears started to recede.

Why be afraid if you are not guilty? Why cry if you are not afraid? Why was she shouting at him? Was it because he had overcome his fear for the first time?

"You better ask Transya, why he picks on me," said Maxim.

"Don't tell me what to do! It's you who are hoping to be admitted to the Pioneers, not Transin."

So, while he was a coward nobody minded, neither the Pioneer Leader nor his classmates, nor the Pioneers from the sixth grade who visited his class. And today, because he behaved like a man for the first time, he could not become a Pioneer?

"Yes, I am going to be a Pioneer," said Maxim.

"Really?" asked Rimma Vasilievna sarcastically.

"Yes, I will," said Maxim in a firm voice. "There was a Pioneer meeting, and they voted for me."

"Well, well! And you think you'll be admitted after I tell them about your behavior?" responded Rimma Vasilievna mockingly.

"I'll also tell them," said Maxim softly, but fearlessly. "And I'll tell them the truth."

"You... mean that I'll tell a lie?"

Maxim did not avert his eyes. His eyes had become used to the sunlight, and now he saw the Pioneer Leader's face.

"Of course," he said in the same a low, but firm voice. "You aren't telling the truth. Why? You just don't like it when somebody argues with you."

"Yes!" said Rimma Vasilievna emphatically and struck the table again. The plate again responded with a jangle. "Yes you are correct! Don't be surprised that I don't like it. Nobody likes it! If everyone like you started to argue with adults it would be the end of the world! The Pioneer Organization is not for brawlers and hooligans, but for obedient children only!"

Maxim suddenly felt that the room had become spacious and empty. As though he stood alone in a great field in a complete silence. And over that field there flew a little red plane. And, remembering the words of the old pilot, Maxim distinctly said in that silence:

"Sheep are obedient, too. But people must fight for the truth."

For several seconds (although it felt like a very long time) Rimma Vasilievna remained sitting as though not understanding what had happened. Then her face stretched, her plucked eyebrows raised up and her mouth opened as if she was going to say: "Ah, that's it! Now it's all clear!"

But she said nothing. Because the forgotten physics teacher let out a chuckle and at once pretended he had a cough. Maxim gave him a quick glance. Physicist as before stood by the window, diligently looking at the street. What did he see there?

Maxim looked at the Pioneer leader again. Now her face was dull and tired.

"Get out of my sight," she said wearily. "A fighter for justice...."

Maxim quickly turned around on the slippery floor and went for the door. He felt that after such words he could not say "Good bye." He closed the door (without a bang, but tightly) and went along the silent, empty corridor.

Maxim was not afraid. He understood that he could be in big trouble, but no fear was in him. He would be a Pioneer anyway! If necessary he would come to the meeting and tell everybody how it really was! Can it be that a person would be refused entry without any reason?

Of course, it was easier for her to argue. She is a Pioneer leader and she is a grown-up. She cried "get out", struck her hand on the table — and the talking was over. But if he was right? Of course, he was right! Justice will win if you are not afraid.

Maxim was walking firmly, his eyes angrily screwed up and fists resolutely clenched. He was not afraid, it was true. Only a vague anxiety was gnawing at him: as though he had forgotten or lost something.

The boltik, that was it!

Maxim stopped. He stood just a second. Then he walked back at the same steady pace. He couldn't give in. If he gave up the boltik it would be a betrayal. The boltik was like a living thing — he had helped it, and it helped him. Now they would throw it away, and it would lay in the garbage alone and useless.

Of course, it was unpleasant to appear again before the infuriated Rimma Vasilievna. Oh, how she would bawl and squall! It was even a little frightening. But Maxim made himself remember the orchestra, and the march "The King of the Sea" was sounding in him again. The trumpet blared and again the shining plates were flung up. And under their ringing clap Maxim pushed open the door.

Rimma Vasilievna and Physicist were arguing about something, standing near the signal trumpets shelf. They immediately stopped talking. The face of the Pioneer leader was resentful, but the teacher reservedly smiled.

The boltik was still lying on the yellow-varnished table. Maxim made five wide steps from the door to the table. He did not lower his eyes. The Pioneer leader and the teacher were watching him with an odd expression on their faces.

"I forgot my boltik," said Maxim loudly. "I'm sorry, but I need it."

Maxim had covered the boltik with his palm and closed his fingers. They felt the usual ribbed weight. Maxim turned around and went back. Nobody said a word to him. And because of this, he delayed on the threshold. He waited until neither a question nor reproach came.

Then, without looking back, he softly said:

"Good bye."

In the corridor he suddenly felt that his legs were feebly trembling. It was even strange because he was not afraid. Yes, really he wasn't. Probably it was because of nervousness. But it's nothing, nervousness is not fear. And once more he made himself walk firmly to the accompaniment of "The King of the Sea" march that started ringing in him again: the persistent song of the trumpets and flashes of the cymbals.

"They can't not admit me!" thought Maxim squeezing the boltik. "They can't! They can't!"

But despite his resoluteness he felt that alarm pricked him again. And once more, stronger.

What was that?

It was because Maxim's way lay by the school's aid post.

"What if they learn that I had lied when I ran away from the vaccination?"

And if they did, it would be the end. He wouldn't see a Pioneer tie for good.

Maxim imagined how it could be: severe reproaches from Sofia Iosifna, scorn from his classmates, a contented look from Rimma Vasilievna: "I told you so...." He even closed his eyes tight, trying to imagine more clearly how things could turn out.... And suddenly he realized and felt: nothing would go wrong. It was he who had imagined all these horrors because of fear living inside him. But now he had none of it. And if there was a little, it was small, shrunken and hidden in the farthest dark corner. That fear feared Maxim itself.

What could happen? Most likely nobody would recall it — they had not done it for two months. But even if they did?

"How could this happen, Rybkin?" they would ask.

"I don't know, I just thought I'd it before."

"What do you mean 'I just thought'?"

"Probably, I got mixed up with last year. And I didn't refuse to be vaccinated. I just warned that I could be vaccinated twice. Well, do it now, if it's necessary."

That would be all, a trifling matter.

But Maxim would go no farther. After all the things that had happened, after choking his fear and becoming a victor, he wanted to chase away the last small fear, too. And unburden his heart from the smear of the lie.

He sighed, shifted from one foot to the other screwing himself up for a desperate confession, and pulled the door!

It did not open.... It was closed!

Let us be perfectly honest: Maxim was not vexed. On the contrary. But his conscience was now clear, and he knew that he would never again tell lies and be afraid. With his heart lightened he skipped down the staircase, looking through a window at the blue sky with a white trace of a jet plane. Suddenly he remembered that he saw the same one over the river, when a plane was piercing the clouds over "The Swallow's Nest."

A new alarm overtook him.

Tanya!

Of course, she would still despise him. Most likely, she was now remembering him, smiling wryly and narrowing her yellow eyes.

He was a coward and braggart! That was how Tanya would remember him.

He had settled up with Transya, but Tanya knew nothing. How would she learn about it? She would be thinking even now that Transya got away with putting on airs, and that Maxim was a coward.

Maxim rushed out from the school and hurried towards the river.

Chapter twelve

"I'll COME TOMORROW!"

The familiar path had brought him back onto the secret ledge. Maxim slipped through the dense, tickling thickness and took a watchful look around. There was silence and nobody in sight; only the withered stalks rustled softly in the wind.

Maxim had got into the crack.

It was pitch darkness. Maxim groped and pulled the string. The bright torch obediently beamed from the ceiling. Nothing had changed since they left. Tanya hadn't been. And she probably wouldn't today.

Maxim sadly sat on the box. When would they meet? And would they meet at all? Of course, Tanya would be thinking, "What a coward, what a coward...." But he wasn't afraid any more! He wasn't the same boy he had been two hours ago.

How could he tell her? Maybe... leave the boltik here? Yes, right! She would arrive and understand everything!

But what if she didn't? What if she thought that mean Vitka Transistor had tracked her down, or what if she imagined something else wrong?

It wouldn't be a bad idea to write her a letter. But how? He had neither a pencil nor paper.... But, maybe there was some paper here? He looked around the walls. The weapon, the Indian headdress, the map.... The small ladies and musketry stood still in their motionless dance. Some plasticine bars lay alongside — to make new warriors and courtiers.

But in olden times ancient people wrote on clay tablets, embossing their letters!

Maxim sprang to his feet and felt the plasticine bars all over: which one was softer? They were equally hard. He chose dark-red, resembling his cherry-colored uniform. He put the boltik aside and kneaded the plasticine until he'd made a round cake.

Maxim squatted down in front of the box, took an

arrow and drew a line on the plasticine. Well, he could write. But what?

"Hi, Tanya! You probably think I was a coward. But I just didn't want to fight because, the day after tomorrow, I should be admitted to the Pioneers, and Rimma Vasilievna could tell people that I am a hooligan.... But then—"

No, it would be a lie. Forget it.

"Hi, Tanya. At first I was afraid to deal with Transya, but when you'd gone—"

No, that was no good either. If he'd stopped being a coward, why recall it? Better this way:

"When you left, I realized that I had to thrash him."

That was better. It was this way indeed: she had left, and then he understood— But it was too long. Maybe, to make it simpler: "I realized that I had to beat him...."

No, that's no good. It should be clearer and shorter.

And, bending down over the plasticine plate, Maxim started scratching words with the arrow tip while the white feather from the arrow flights swept widely over his field cap. And he wrote:

Thrashed him
Will come here tomorrow at 2 o'clock
Maxim

Then he thought, "What if she comes later?" But he reassured himself at once, "No, she'll be on time! And if not, I'll leave her another note."

Next to the plasticine plate Maxim laid the boltik — the witness of his victory. And at once he felt sympathy for it: it would be bored alone, in the darkness.

Maxim took it again, sighed, pressed it to his chest... and then he had an inspired idea! He turned the boltik over and made an imprint on the plasticine. The flat head with an accurate number "12" printed off, next to his name, like a real stamp. Although, the number had appeared back to front, but Tanya would guess anyway.

Suddenly he heard a rustling noise coming from outside. Big drops started flicking on the leaves, and the entrance became curtained with glassy strings. The sun was still shining, but a small cloud had gathered in the sky and poured down the first summer rain. As if it wanted to play a joke on Maxim and keep him in "The Swallow's Nest."

He didn't get angry with the cloud. The cheerful sound of the raindrops and their sparkling in the sun were telling him that soon it would be over. And yes, in two minutes the rain had passed over, leaving the grass on the ledge glassy and glinting. And over the dove-colored cloud there appeared a steep, bright rainbow. Or rather, two rainbows — one inside the other. These multicolored gates were reflecting in the water as blurred stripes, until a white hydrofoil speedboat tore them to pieces.

Maxim got out and went up the path. The clay became slippery; the blades of grass caught his legs with their little wet palms. His shirtsleeves got wet, too, from brushing against the wet grass. But it was nothing, and was even pleasant.

The sky had already cleared; the little cloud was stealing away beyond the river, its ragged edge glowing gold. The opposite shore shone with wet roofs and windowpanes. It was very easy to breathe. And it even seemed that if you jumped from a cliff you wouldn't fall down, but fly upwards like a bird.

Sliding on his sandals, Maxim climbed up onto the high riverbank and stood on the edge. He got a little tired, but felt cheerful and relaxed, because he had done everything just as it should have been done.

After the rain the air smelled of poplar freshness. Maxim felt so good that he wanted to hug a poplar growing nearby. To hug it and say "thank you" for this summer evening, for the recent warm rain, for the rainbow. For his joy and victory.

And so he did. No longer concerned that he could stain his cherry-colored uniform, he hugged the rough, gray trunk and pressed it with his cheek, chest and knees. He stood, merging with the tree and listening to the summer.

There came a light wind, and the branches started swaying. A big, warm drop fell down on Maxim's temple and ran over his cheek. He smiled and closed his eyes.

Somebody touched Maxim's shoulder lightly. He tore his cheek away from the trunk and slowly turned around.

Before him stood a man. Maxim looked at him from his feet upwards, and, probably because of this, he didn't recognize him right away. Then he realized that it was the physics teacher.

Maxim was neither surprised nor worried. He just thought, "Here is the physics teacher again." Inwardly, Maxim was still smiling, but he gave the teacher a serious look. Serious and calm.

"Were you crying?" asked the teacher softly.

Maxim shook his head.

"But what's this?" said Physicist and touched Maxim's cheek with his little finger — there remained a wet track.

Maxim smiled again. A little.

"That's a drop from the tree," he explained and glanced at the leaves.

Physicist did, too.

Then they looked at each other.

"I thought you were crying," said the teacher in the same quiet voice. "Don't take offence. It happens, sometimes, that a man is brave while it's necessary, but then he cries when he's alone. Because of resentment or tiredness."

"I know. But I wasn't crying. I didn't even feel like it," said Maxim.

"Good for you, then. So, give me your hand and let's go."

"Where?" queried Maxim.

"Where.... You should go home, I suppose. What are you doing here, in the evening?"

"I was... playing," Maxim said and looked aside. Physicist was a good man, and he didn't want to tell a lie or invent things. "There's a secret place here," he explained and raised his eyes again. "But it's not my secret, so don't ask me about it."

Physicist nodded:

"I won't.... Although, I must admit, you'd frightened me with your secret."

"Me? How?"

"How.... You see, you rushed out... well, you went out, so angry, so resolute. I also set off home. And I saw you going ahead of me. It so happened that we were on the same path. Then I saw — you go to the river. I thought maybe you'd decided to jump headlong into the water.... Well, I was joking, of course," laughed Physicist hurriedly. "But anyway, it was strange: you went down and disappeared without a trace. You must agree, anybody would have started to worry...."

"Yes, perhaps," said Maxim, after thinking it over. "But I didn't know you were there."

"It's all right now," said Physicist. "Well, now, what about going home?"

He held out his hand, and Maxim took it with his free hand, not with the one in which he clutched the boltik. The teacher kept Maxim's pace, and they walked rather slowly. Maxim cast quick glances at Physicist, thinking this was the first time he'd been out holding a teacher's hand, while not on an excursion. It was interesting, what was his name? It would be awkward to ask. He would find out at home from Andrew. And in three years' time Maxim would study physics himself, and perhaps he would meet this teacher every day. It was a pity that Rimma Vasilievna was the Pioneer leader, and not him.

"And about the Pioneer meeting, don't worry," said Physicist unexpectedly. "Everything will be all right."

"I'm not worried," answered Maxim and again felt that he had told a lie. "No, I am worried, but I'm not afraid," he checked himself, and angrily screwed up his eyes.

"That's good," smiled the teacher.

"Of course, it's good," Maxim said independently and shot a proud glance at Physicist.

But his anxiety appeared to be stronger than his pride. And he asked softly:

"But... is it true that everything will be all right?"

"Yes," said Physicist.

And this firm "yes" banished Maxim's awakened alarm completely. His pace had inadvertently changed. If he were alone, he would probably start skipping with joy. But Physicist held his hand so Maxim just smiled.

"What's wrong? Does your leg hurt?" asked Physicist,

and he glanced at Maxim's bandage.

"No, it doesn't hurt at all!"

"You're a tough cookie," said Physicist with respect. "As tough as your boltik."

"Why tough? My leg really doesn't hurt."

"Well, I trust your word. OK, here's my street, I have to turn off here. Good bye, Boltik."

"Good bye...," replied Maxim. And when the teacher was already five steps away, Maxim ventured to ask:

"What's your name?"

Perhaps it was not very polite to ask like that, when someone wasn't looking at you. If Mama were here, she would certainly have scolded him. But Physicist turned around, as though he was expecting this question.

"My name's Roman Sergeevich. Why do you ask?"

"Well.... Do you know Andrew Rybkin, from 9a?"

"Yes, I do," said Roman Sergeevich seriously. "He's a very able young man."

"He's my brother," said Maxim with pleasure.

"You don't say! Well, that is very nice. My greetings to Andrew Rybkin. By the way, his class will be having a test the day after tomorrow."

"Will you be teaching us in the sixth grade?"

"I hope so.... If nothing untoward happens."

"But what could happen?" asked Maxim anxiously.

"Who knows," teased Roman Sergeevich. "Maybe they'll appoint me Chief of the Department of Education."

"Oh! Could they? Maybe they won't," Maxim reassured him.

Roman Sergeevich laughed, waved his hand and walked down his street.

Chapter thirteen

HAVE YOU FALLEN FROM THE SKY?

The evening sun was shining on Maxim's back, and a long, slim-legged shadow was striding comically ahead of him. It limped slightly, because Maxim was limping too: his knee had begun hurting again. Besides that, his shoulder ached from the hard blow from Transya. His tiredness fluctuated in him like heavy water.

But don't think that Maxim was walking crest-fallen. It was only his pace that was slow. He was in good spirits, anyway. Maxim smiled: ahead of him there was nothing but good.

Well, there was one thing that was not very nice: Mama would probably be cross to see Maxim's scruffy appearance.

Walking past the bakery Maxim cast a glance at his reflection in the shop window. Well.... Certainly not all his feathers were in place. His shirt cuffs and sleeves were gray, and the shorts looked as though they had been chewed up. His legs were bruised and scratched all over, as if he had fought with a pack of jungle cats. And the bandage! It was even difficult to believe that once it was white.

But, well, it's nothing! He would be coming back as a victor, and they say success is never criticized. Especially since his field cap was still sitting on his head, as new.

Maxim swallowed hard and hurriedly left. Because he had seen, apart from himself, bread sticks and roasted round loaves behind the glass. He really felt lightheaded from hunger. How great it would be to find himself at home, right now. What a pity he had no strength to run.

At the corner of the street there was a cart with a sign saying "Pies." A wrinkled, old saleswoman, wearing a white overall and cap, was bending down over her box, rustling some wrapping paper. Maxim went up, with his mouth watering, and held out his five rubles.

"Please give me—"

She straightened up so quickly that Maxim had no time to finish.

"No change, I've turned over the cash! Can't you see I am closing?"

No, he couldn't see it. He saw only the pies — big-bellied, the color of gold. They lay piled in an aluminum tray. They were probably filled with meat or rice. But, after all, he wouldn't die! Better to bear the hunger than to stay and beg.

Maxim shrugged his shoulders and walked away, trying not to limp. And behind him, he could hear the woman's grumbling:

"Just look at him — such a small chap, with all that money...."

Where do they come from such spiteful people? This one, Marina, or that woman behind the fence when Maxim was chopping the burdock with his chip....

"Boy!" he suddenly heard the same voice. "Boy, wait!"

What else did she want? To question him, asking where he took the money from? It was none of her business.

Maxim stopped and looked back.

"Boy," said the saleswoman, not angrily. "Come here."

He shrugged his shoulders again and came up.

"Take it," said the saleswoman and held out a pie in a paper serviette.

"Oh, why, no need," said Maxim embarrassed and feeling that he was turning red.

"Take, take it and don't be cross."

Now she was not spiteful at all. She smiled and looked a bit guilty.

Maxim wanted to say "Thank you, I don't want it," but the pie was so amazingly tempting, that his hand stretched out to it by itself. And his tongue by itself said:

"Thank you very much...."

"Help yourself, please. Don't take offence at me, an old grumbler. I've been here all day in the sun. I am completely done in!"

Maxim said "thank you" once more and walked away, casting back surprised glances.

How strange.... Was she angry or kind? Good or bad?

Maybe even Marina was not bad after all? Maybe she had had a hard life with her Vitya, the drunkard....

But anyway. If you feel bad, why throw yourself at those who are not guilty of causing it? Why think that everybody else is bad, too?

For instance, Ivan Savelyevich's life was also difficult, but he understands at once who is bad, and who is not.

"5-5, Gromov Street" — Maxim would certainly visit him. And maybe Ivan Savelyevich would ask his friends, the pilots, to give Maxim a ride on a plane....

Of course, he would!! And they, of course, would agree! If a man is kind, his friends must be kind, too.

Good people always come to rescue and help. Luba, the nurse; Roman Sergeevich, the teacher.... And Tanya!

Tomorrow Maxim would certainly go to the shore. Good people can say just a word, and you feel much better. For instance, that blue-eyed old man, who had given him the chip. Or the guard-woman from the TV center....

If Maxim could, he would also do something good for them, in return. Certainly!

Only what could he do? Just sing a little. If only it were possible to arrange one more concert and compose a really good song for them! So that they knew it was for them....

The wind was also kind. It was dense and very warm. It came from the direction of the sun and pushed Maxim gently in his back, helping him to walk.

The pie had disappeared. Maxim had even licked the crumbs. There remained only a sweet reminiscence of the meat stuffing and the thin roasted crust. His hunger remained, too. It was teased even more. What was a small pie for such a huge hunger? Papa would say, "It's like a pellet for an elephant."

For an elephant....

"Buy an elephant," he recalled.

Maxim smiled and went to Grizodubova Street[1]. He had never walked along that street, but knew that it must lead him almost to his home. It must be the shortest way.

---

[1] *Valentina Grizodubova, the first female pilot in the USSR (—Tr.)*

But he had serious doubts when the street came to an end after two blocks, leading him to a gray, shaky fence.

What should he do? He could not see any way around the fence. But turning back was such a long way....

Some planks were torn off. An elephant certainly would not squeeze through that hole, but Maxim slipped easily into the crack: maybe there was a path there?

There was. The path snaked through the high grass, crossing open wasteland, or maybe it was an abandoned stadium. On one edge of the area there was a lopsided football gate, and on the other, a wooden shed or garage. The sun was still above the horizon, hiding behind high-rise buildings and covering the wasteland with a blue evening shadow.

The wind was steadily rustling in the grass. From the nearby airfield could be heard the thrumming of engines.

Maxim walked on along the path, towards the shed. Maxim thought it was completely abandoned, but when he went up closer he heard voices.

And at that moment, three boys rolled out a strange contraption on small, different caliber wheels. Maxim was a few steps away, but the boys did not notice him, because at first they were bent over, messing about with their rattletrap construction. And then they stood up and cast thoughtful looks towards it.

Maxim stood waist-deep in the old grass. He didn't know what to do. Unknown boys — it was a risk. But the path went next to them. If he went around, through the grass, they could say that he was hanging about and following them. Maybe he should turn around and go away unnoticed? But where could he go? And, besides, it would be cowardice again.

But why should he be afraid? It was clear, the boys were not bad people. They were happily occupied. The youngest was about seven, fair-haired, thin, big-eyed. He faintly resembled somebody Maxim had met before, but he could not recall whom. The two others were probably from the sixth or seventh grade. One was stocky, with dark freckles on his sharp cheekbones; the other was almost as tall as an adult, but narrow-shouldered and with a thin neck. The wind was ruffling his fluffy hair.

Their faces were serious and thoughtful. The stocky boy was scratching his chin, and the little one took quick, anxious glances first at him then at the tall boy.

Maxim decided that he could go on without fear. But it was awkward to go by without saying any word, as if it were an empty place. And... well, it was really interesting, what they were doing.

Maxim plucked up his courage and asked:

"And what have you made?"

They immediately looked at him.

The stocky boy left his chin alone and said with surprise:

"Dear me! Have you fallen from the sky?"

The tall boy smiled, and his smile was amicable. But his voice was unexpectedly high pitched:

"From the sky, indeed. Look, he's a pilot."

"No, he isn't a pilot," said the little boy in an all-knowing tone. "He's from the Palace, the musician group. My brother Venka also has a similar uniform, but a bit different."

"Vladik, where's your Venka?" asked the stocky boy angrily. "He promised to fetch some wire...."

"Ah, there's no wire," said the boy, carelessly. "He didn't find any. He'll be here soon himself, after watching television. There's something important on."

"Important!" said the stocky boy with a frown. "He's promised, but now what? What'll we fasten the steering wheel with?"

"He's promised nothing, Oleg. He said that he'd look for it. Should he search until his death if he'd found nothing?" said the little boy emphatically.

Then, as if remembering Maxim, they looked at him again.

"Is it a kind of automobile?" asked Maxim.

The installation was made of iron pipes, strips of wood and stood on three wheels: the two rear wheels were taken from a small bicycle, and the front wheel, from a children's scooter. Most of all it resembled a mock-up of one of the first automobiles. However, the rear wheels were located too far from each other.

"Uh-huh, an automobile. With an atomic engine,"

responded the stocky Oleg.

The tall boy smiled:

"Stop it...." And he explained without any mocking airs and graces: "This is a yacht on wheels. With a sail. Here..." and he pointed at a long pole that lay near the wall. It was wrapped with gray fabric, and Maxim realized it was a sail.

"And will it go?" he asked.

"It will. Especially in the wind like today...."

"And if we find some wire," said Oleg angrily.

The little boy poked with his finger into an iron loop in the little wheel axis and explained, looking seriously at Maxim:

"We need to fasten it with wire here, so the steering wheel won't come off. That's the main thing now."

Maxim took a close look.

"What about fastening it with a screw?"

"Where would you get one?" said the tall boy with a gesture of annoyance. "There are none, as ill luck would have it. Vladik's rummaged around all the scrap-heaps today."

This could be seen very well because the front of Vladik's blue tee shirt, the knees of his jeans and even his cheeks were all covered in rust.

Well, there was nothing for it. Everything was fitting into place. Of course, Maxim had become used to the boltik and loved it, but the boltik could not live in his fist all the time. It must be in its proper place and be of use. And its most proper place was here, near the steering wheel.

Maxim sighed and opened his palm.

"Will this one be right?"

They all stared at the boltik. And at once they started smiling, even gloomy Oleg. And the tall boy said:

"Wow, you fell from sky indeed! You're our rescuer."

And bumping their heads, they bent over the wheel and started adjusting the boltik. Maxim squatted down next to them. Little Vladik glanced at him and said:

"Venka will be so glad."

"Certainly he resembles somebody I've seen before," thought Maxim again. "Maybe I met his brother in the ensemble. It's interesting, I wonder which group he attends?" But it was awkward to ask.

"We appeared on television today," he said, and it sounded as if he was talking about himself and Venka together.

"Venka told us, but we didn't watch it," replied the tall boy. "There was so much work, and we forgot. We've been messing around with this thing since this morning."

He straightened up and looked at Maxim from his height.

"Well, thank you for the screw. We'll give you a ride, for sure. What's your name?"

"Maxim."

The tall boy blinked perplexedly.

"Really? I am Maxim, too!"

That was great! As if they almost became friends.

"We'll give you a ride, as much as you like," repeated the tall Maxim.

"When should I come?"

"As soon as we start testing it we'll call you, straightaway," said Oleg unexpectedly. "We could do with one more person. And you're a decent chap."

Inside Maxim felt a warm wave of gratitude.

"And when will you test it?" he asked.

"Tomorrow," said the tall Maxim. "Today we'll rig it, and tomorrow morning, weigh anchor.... If the wind doesn't drop."

"No, this wind won't drop," said Vladik determinedly. And Maxim believed him.

"Well, by the way, where do you live?" the tall Maxim suddenly remembered. "How will we find you?"

"I live in Technikov Street[1]. House number 3, flat 40. The second entrance."

"Oh, it's near," said Oleg.

"Is it?" replied Maxim uncertainly. "I don't know.... We've moved here recently. I was going along Grizodubova Street, and it just disappeared."

The boys laughed. The tall Maxim said:

"No it didn't. Go through this gate, and it continues

---

[1] or Technician Street

there. And your street's a block farther.... So, your house is number 3, flat 40?"

"Yes, it is," said Maxim. "Only don't forget.... I've to go."

The sun had already disappeared below the horizon, and Maxim suddenly realized that at home they were probably worrying about him.

"Bye," said Oleg and stretched out his hand.

And the tall Maxim, too.

And little Vladik also stretched his little palm, dirty with rust.

Chapter fourteen

LIGHT IN THE GRASS

What do all mothers say when their sons appear after the promised time, crumpled, disheveled and with battle scratches? They always say the same words:

"My goodness! Where have you been loitering about? Why do you look like such a ragamuffin?!"

What do their sons say? They ought to sigh contritely, lower their eyes and show with all their appearance that they are very upset, and that things have happened quite accidentally, and, the main thing, that it won't happen again. Then it is possible to avoid a telling-off or, at least, to weaken it.

But the joy of a victor was still ringing in Maxim despite his tiredness, and replying to Mama's words, he rather indiscreetly said:

"Today was such a day..." and looked at Mama with happy eyes.

Mama asked stiffly what was special about today and where had he been hanging about all day. Certainly, no excursion could last from morning to evening.

"Why from morning to evening?" said Maxim with a slightly offended tone. "At first was the concert, then—"

"So, you are going to tell us that you've been to the TV

center?"

"But where else was I?" wondered Maxim. "Why, haven't you seen the concert on television? Have you?"

"Well, do you know...," said Papa. "It's no way for a real man to dodge like this. Are you really going to tell us about a television concert when there hasn't been any concert?"

Maxim glanced at Papa and then at Mama. They were not joking.

"What are you talking about!" said Maxim loudly. "You've just missed the broadcast and now you tell me that I'm a fibber!"

"How dare you be so rude!" exclaimed Mama. "It exceeds all the limits! Isn't it enough that you are feeding us with stories; then you also raise your voice!"

"Me? Telling stories?" asked Maxim softly.

Why is a human organism organized in such a mean way? When the truth is on your side, and you must speak calmly and proudly, your throat starts filling with prickly crumbs, your eyes start itching and there appear creepy drops....

"Well who's telling stories, then? Maybe we are?"

"You've simply mixed up the time."

"No, we haven't. On the local television there was news and a concert, but not yours — it was a folklore ensemble from Moscow. And on Moscow's channel there were morning exercises and 'People and Law.' That's all."

"Maybe our TV set is broken!"

Mama gave a laugh with an unpleasant tone of voice:

"That's just wonderful! It's broken and turned your chorus into a folklore ensemble!"

"Our TV set is perfectly in order," said Papa. He was even not too lazy to stand up and solemnly turn the switch on. "Look, it works like clockwork."

Maxim did not look at it. He turned around and limped to the kitchen. There was an appetizing smell of the hot dinner. But his appetite had gone. All that had happened extinguished his former joy and weighed Maxim down like a heavy load upon his shoulders.

First, there was no concert on TV!

Second, how could he have said the silly words about

a broken TV set?

And third, why didn't they believe him? Had he ever told them lies or hid his mark book when he got bad marks? If he did something wrong he never denied it. There were many things Maxim was afraid of, but never was he afraid of his mama and papa. Of course, it happened that he was scolded hard, but it was always just. Only once Mama gave him a cuff on the back of his neck for a broken teapot (Papa had then told her in a whisper: "Tut-tut! And you graduated from a teachers' training college that disapproves of hitting children?"). But that anger would just be for a moment. Then they would take pity on him and forgive him.

Why didn't they believe him?

Maxim sat down at the table and laid his head on his crossed hands. The saucepan of soup gently warmed his cheek.

Maxim gulped several times and choked his tears down. But a bitter feeling remained.

"Maybe it was just a rehearsal, and they weren't told?" said Papa in the room.

"Oh, stop it!" argued Mama. "It's just his fantasy's exceeded the limits. It happens sometimes at his age."

"Nowhere has it exceeded," said Maxim.

"Stop eavesdropping!" Mama raised her voice.

"I am not eavesdropping. You yourselves are talking loudly.... And if you don't believe me, phone up Anatoly Fedorovich...."

"'Rehearsal,'" thought Maxim angrily, "then, they would have told us when the real concert would be. And why did he need to turn on the TV cameras?"

But maybe it was a dream, indeed? The studio, the song.... And the orchestra, and the boy with cymbals?

Why did he recall that boy again and again? Maybe, because of his cymbals? They were so shiny and gave out such a great pealing ring that it made the march sound stronger and better....

And the march echoed in Maxim again. Loudly and confidently. Maxim even wondered and raised his head.

No, it was not sounding in his imagination. It was in the drawing room! Limping on his left leg he skipped to the door.

On the TV screen there was an orchestra. THAT VERY ONE! And the boy-musician was raising his cymbals and then moved them smoothly apart. He was framed in a close-up, to the waist. The cymbals flared so brightly that the TV set screen failed to show their glitter properly, making it almost black. And the boy's forelock merrily stood on end after every clash.

He looked out without a smile, and only in his eyes there were cheery dots. He looked right at Maxim! As if he came to help him.

"That's our folk!" shouted Maxim. "It's us! Here! Hurray!"

"It means.... Ah, well, it's clear now!" exclaimed Papa and looked at them as if he had made a discovery. "Of course! Why did you think that it would be a direct transmission? As a rule, they record it and then show it!"

The march was ringing. The victorious march! Maxim was looking at the screen with his eyes shining.

"Have you been on, yet?" asked Mama in an alarmed voice.

"No, no. It'll be later...."

"Maxim," Papa said seriously, "we were wrong. Please, forgive us."

"Well, OK," said Maxim impatiently. "Let's watch. It's all interesting."

He skipped to the sofa and climbed on with his feet, next to Papa. Mama turned the chandelier off, and the TV screen became brighter in the soft light of the standard lamp.

The boy clashed his cymbals for the last time, and the march ended. The audience started applauding. Maxim saw himself: one of his hands was busy with the boltik, and he was clapping with his fist against the opened palm. Mama and Papa had also seen him. Mama even said, "Oh, dear!" But at that moment the dance group appeared....

... Everything was exactly like at the concert. They had even shown how "The Little Wings" were running on the stage. And again Maxim saw himself! But he took a place behind Ritka Penkina, and when they were singing

"The Grasshopper", only his field cap could be seen. Oh well, never mind....

Then Alex Tigritsky appeared. He put his hands behind his back, nodded to the pianist and started singing.

"What a nice voice he's got," said Mama. "What a wonderful, healthy child. Not like ours, skinny as a toothpick."

"Humph! Do you really want Maxim to be as round as him?" asked Papa in an indignant whisper.

"Hush! Let's watch!" said Maxim pitifully.

Alex had finished his song and bowed importantly.

Maxim's heart missed a beat. Because now, now....

"The song 'The First Flight!' The soloist is Maxim Rybkin!"

Oh, gosh! Was it possible that it was him? So little, disheveled, with scared eyes! His field cap, it's true, was in its place, but the waistcoat buttons looked off-center. The shorts were uneven, too: one leg was longer than the other— Bang! He stumbled and nearly knocked Margarita Penkina onto the floor.

"Oh, hippopotamus...," whispered Mama with a groan.

Maxim shrank. Why did he look like that? Why did he have a blank look and give confused glances? And moving his lips.... Were they real fools in the studio? Why did they show at all on screen how he was squeezing his fist with the boltik? You could also see that his other hand was timidly fingering the edge of his shorts, and the button on his cuff was undone....

"Stop squeezing your boltik, silly!" muttered Maxim under his breath.

"Don't worry, don't worry, Maxim," said Papa. He was speaking to the Maxim who was on the TV screen. But there was no reason now to say, "Don't worry!" Too late....

Again they showed his face. Why did he knit his brows and look right at the camera, stupid?

Gosh, it was a terrible, undeniable flop! How awful it would be if the children from his class were watching the concert, too. What laughter there would be on Monday! What a present for Transya!

The chorus started singing.... Oh, it was no use now!

Nothing but a humiliation. The only good thing was that now they were showing not him, but the other children....

> *"The sun has just arisen*
> *A breeze has touched the grass...."*

Oh, how did they do that? On the screen there appeared a field with daisy flowers; the grass was quivering. A small plane stood on the grass. And a boy was going through this grass towards the plane. He resembled Maxim. Probably, it was taken from some movie.

And, through this field of daisies, Maximka's face slowly appeared. Now, he neither beetled his brows nor moved his lips. He was tensely looking out from the screen and waiting. And then he started singing.

He was singing, asking for a flight. It did not sound pitiful, but rather, with an intense, relentless persistence. Maxim had never thought that he had such a voice. It was completely unknown. It was not as high and clear as Alex's, but it was ringing. It was a desperate, ringing demand for a miracle!

What was going on — they showed his eyes again. Full screen. Why? And right in his eyes there was the running boy again and the sparkling circle of the propeller.... Then, Maxim again, to his full height.

> *"...I often dream of it in the night*
> *Take me, I'm very light!"*

Papa softly coughed. And on the screen there appeared a curly boy from the audience. He was sitting leaning forward, biting his lip. Of course, he sympathized with Maxim. Probably he felt awkward because of him.

But then.... Why was he feeling so strange, seeing the flowing grass under the soaring plane and the propeller glittering in the sun? And as though hearing his thoughts the chorus gaily responded:

"The plane with the boy rushed on and took off!
Higher!
Higher...
Higher...."

The song became silent. The plane had hidden in the sun. And Maxim became quiet, too; only his heart was pulsating like a machine-gun....

"My little boy...," said Papa softly and turned to Mama: "Here! Just look what a son we've got!"

And Mama took him tenderly by his ears and kissed him on his nose.

What was that? It meant they weren't ashamed of him? It meant... it wasn't bad after all?

At that moment the TV set burst into the noise of stormy applause. Maxim started.

Of course! It had all taken place already today!

Over there, at the TV center, was his victory, and he stood there happy and overwhelmed — the same as he was now on the TV screen. How could he forget it? He had felt so ashamed of the way the song started that he had forgotten about the end! But here was the end! Everybody was clapping — the children from the chorus, unknown boys and girls. And that boy-musician, too! Maxim had not seen him from the stage, but now here he was! And he was clapping so hard that his forelock stood on end again.

Could it be that he, Maxim, gave him this joy? To him and to the others....

Now on the stage there appeared Anatoly Fedorovich and the girl with the microphone.

"Your name's Maxim, isn't? My congratulations, Maxim; you sang very well. Didn't he, children?"

"... It's your first appearance on stage, isn't?"

"... What are you going to be, Maxim?"

Ah, why did he look so stupid? Well, not stupid, but so confused....

"... And what is in your fist?"

"It's... only one thing, a boltik...."

"How interesting. But why did you take it?"

"It's for firmness...," and his palm is shown at half screen! With the boltik!

Everybody is clapping, nobody laughs. Except Mama. She embraced Maxim and said through her laughter, squeezing his shoulders:

"In full view, like a cake on the plate! Oh, Maxim, Maxim! Even there you've shown what a junkman you are!"

But she said it kindly. And Maxim laughed and began swinging his legs, because it appeared that everything was great.

Mama caught his leg.

"Well, now stop swinging and tell me why you are bandaged, all covered in clay. Tell me everything that has happened to you."

"Only after dinner," groaned Maxim. "Or I'll die of hunger."

"Then off you go to wash your hands."

"U-u-uh...."

"What does that mean 'u-uh?'"

"Ma," said Maxim playfully, "buy an elephant."

"Which elephant...? What next? One's begging for a tape recorder, another, for an elephant."

"Everybody asks 'Which elephant?'" said Maxim pensively, "but you go and buy it."

"I am asking seriously—"

"Everybody says 'I am asking seriously,'" interrupted Maxim. "But you don't ask. Just go and buy it."

Mama looked at Papa. He was looking at Maxim biting his lip.

"I don't understand—" started Mama.

"Everybody says 'I don't understand.' But you just buy it."

Mama smiled:

"Everybody says, 'Buy an elephant!' And nobody wants to wash his hands. Off you go to the bathroom, or I'll help you with my broom!"

Maxim burst out laughing and went out.

Then he sat at the table and ate. He ate his lunch, dinner and supper. Soup, frankfurters and cooked semolina with jam. Then he drank his tea with "Kitty-kitty" toffees and told his tale. Of the concert. Of the guard-woman's gun. Of the iron, the third floor, the transom and Marina.

"You deserve a good thrashing," said Mama pitifully. "But what if you had broken your neck?"

"But what if the whole house had burnt down?"

"A human life costs more than a house!"

"It's a question of honor and self-esteem," said Papa.

"That's a question of foolishness," said Mama.

"Well, nothing's happened," said Maxim, "it's all over now."

Mama expressed a hope that in the future Maxim would not take risks so stupidly.

Maxim said "yes," just in case, and told them about Ivan Savelyevich; then, incidentally, about being vaccinated and, finally, how Marina had appeared and how she had been driven away by Ivan Savelyevich.

"Well, well," said Mama. "What a wild day you've had— Stop gobbling toffees or you'll burst.... And your leg should be bandaged afresh. Does it hurt?"

"Nope."

"And where did this clay come from?"

"I was walking to the park along the river and got bogged down near a brook. I thought I would get dirty all over, but a girl helped...."

"Well, I hope you thanked her?"

"Yeah, then we played together. She has a secret place on the shore...."

"But why on earth did you go to the river bank? Or is that a secret, too?"

Maxim had no time to answer. Andrew had arrived.

"A reveler!" said Mama. "You've missed Maxim's concert! It ended just a short while ago."

"No, I didn't," responded Andrew, "I was at Galka Jilcova's. Our Maxim isn't a child, but a great actor. Keep that in mind Maxim, Galka fell in love with you."

"Oh, I need her as much as a cat needs kerosene."

"And also, Maxim has told us about his exploits," remarked Papa.

"Has he already told you how he switched off Transistor?"

(Gosh, how did he know?)

"Oh, stop talking like that, at least at home," said Mama. "And it was not a transistor, but a clothes iron."

"No, it was exactly Transistor, a good-for-nothing from the fourth grade. And he literally switched him off. To be more exact, he gave him a bloody nose and black eye."

"Maxim, have you been fighting?" asked Mama with her eyes wide open.

"What else could I do — he's always picking on me first! If he fights me again, he'll get more."

"Only don't start first," suggested Andrew. "It sometime happens: when a person has felt his strength, he begins venting his anger on everybody around. Transya began like that."

"I am not Transya," said Maxim jauntily.

Then he went to the room he shared with Andrew to read the new edition of the Pioneers newspaper. But he made a mistake. He should have turned on the light and then flopped down on the sofa. But he had flopped down first and now he felt too lazy to stand up. Behind the window the noise of the wind could be heard. It was shaking the branches, and the twilight in the room was rocking like a dark, luminescent sea. Maxim put the paper aside and simply lay there, looking at the wall.

... When you peer into twilight you can see different pictures. It may be giants, ancient cities, ships in the sea.... Maxim had seen a jungle. And he walked warily through the tufts of palm leaves, lianas and high grass. He came out at the clearing. There stood a huge, gray elephant. Maxim stepped back. The elephant had seen him. It stood up on its hind legs and gently ran towards Maxim, throwing out its stomach. Maxim ran away.

"Wait, wait!" blared the elephant with the voice of Ivan Savelyevich. "Where are you going? Don't be afraid."

Maxim recalled that he was not a coward any more and stopped.

The elephant came right over to Maxim, and its huge, round belly overhung him like an airship Ivan Savelyevich had flown on in his youth.

"Where are you going?" repeated the elephant. "Such a little boy, but so crafty! You've bought me, and now you are running away."

"You say, I've bought you?" said Maxim gingerly.

"Yes, of course! You asked your mama and she agreed."

"But where can I put you?"

"Everybody says, 'Where can I put you?'" said the elephant pensively. "Think for yourself as you've bought me."

"But how can I feed you?"

"Everybody says 'How can I feed you?' You'll feed me with toffees, of course!"

"Well, OK," said Maxim, "I'll settle you down somewhere behind the garages...."

"No, I don't like it there," sighed the elephant again. "Better, I'll live here. And you can visit me. Don't forget the toffees...."

Maxim was glad and wanted to say that he wouldn't forget, but suddenly heard the doorbell....

Maxim opened his eyes. The elephant had disappeared, and again there was the dusk of the room.

The doorbell rang out again. It seemed Mama had opened the door. Maxim heard:

"Who do you want, boys?"

"How do you do? Please can you tell us, does Maxim live here?"

"Yes, he does.... But it's already too late. It seems he's turned in and he's dead asleep."

"No, I am not!" said Maxim rushing out of the door. Because he had recognized the voices. There on the doorstep were Oleg, the tall Maxim and Vladik.

"We've come for you," said the tall Maxim. "Everything's ready."

Mama gasped:

"What is ready at this time of night?"

"Just something interesting," said Maxim hurriedly. "We need to test it, while the wind holds. Yes, boys?"

Mama wanted to say that Maxim would go nowhere, but... she met with his eyes. And she had probably realized that today's Maxim had become much more mature than yesterday's. She gave a glance at Papa, sighed and looked at the boys again.

And then small, big-eyed Vladik said:

"Oh, please, don't worry. We'll see him back."

Mama gave a soft laugh and waved her hand.

"Only no longer than half an hour."

The triangle wing of the mainsail was fluttering over the darkened grass in the blue evening air. It seemed to be alive.

"Sit down," said Oleg. "Hold the rope. And when you hear 'release the brake' — press this thing." And he put Maximka's hand on a wooden lever.

The lever was smooth and warm.

Maxim settled himself on the narrow plank, next to the left wheel. With his right hand he seized the wire stretched down from the top of the mast. There, over the mast and the trembling edge of the mainsail, he caught sight of a glittering bright star. It was as though somebody had hung up a faceted Christmas tree toy and it was spinning in the wind.

The star was alone; the evening was still light. A yellowish clear sunset was burning out in the west.

However, the distant houses and fences had already blended into a dark mass. And now it was unclear whether the clearing was big or small and how far the runway would be. From this uncertainty and expectation there came a slight anxiety.

A bright torch had turned on and flickered several times in the bushes to the left of the football gate (Maxim recalled Tanya and "The Swallow's Nest").

"Now!" cried little Vladik.

He sat down in front, and the tall Maxim on the side next to the right wheel.

Oleg had stood up behind the yacht.

"Hey, pull up the clew line...."

"Aye-aye!" the tall Maxim said.

The big sail had stopped fluttering and bent resiliently under the force of the wind. Maxim could feel its tight vibration through the wire. The yacht had lurched. Maxim's throat became dry.

"Release the brake!"

"Aye-aye!" cried Maxim and raised the lever.

Something had clicked under the wheel. Oleg pushed the yacht and jumped on the rear seat. They started moving, slowly at first. The yacht jolted over some mounds. And some more and more.... The speed was increasing fast, and the yacht started clinking with its tightened wires. The brittle grass stalks lashed Maxim's legs. Then he felt that he was smoothly lifting up. The left wheel took off from the ground! Maxim softly cried out: he thought that now they would keel over. But the yacht kept running with the heeling on the right side, and the left wheel flew over the tops of the grass, gradually slowing its rotation.

And it was not scary at all. It was fun! To spare his legs Maxim at first dragged them to his chin, and then, obeying his joyous mood, sprang up to his feet!

Clenching the thin guy line, he was flying over the grass — right to the place with the shining torch. The warm wind was beating on his left shoulder; the wide sleeves of his shirt were fluttering on his elbows.

It was like a flight! Like a great song!

They seemed to fly very-very long....

The torch flashed from the left.

"Sit down!" cried Oleg. "We are turning!"

Maxim barely had time to squat down when a sudden force pressed him to the mast. The boom of the sail had rushed over his head. The sail flapped and got tightened again. The left wheel started jumping over the ground. The yacht was running past the football gate. The torch again was sparkling ahead.

"Break up!" shouted Oleg. "Press!"

Maxim thrust upon the lever with his elbow.

The yacht stopped so abruptly that the mast rocked ahead, and Maxim couldn't hold onto his place and fell head over heels onto the grass.

The boys picked him up and seated him on the ground.

"Are you alive? Are you all right?"

"I am fine!" said Maxim happily.

"Next time, don't press the lever so hard. Do it smoothly...."

This was spoken not by the tall Maxim or Oleg and not by Vladik either. It was the boy that had just signaled them with the torch. He was now twiddling it with his hand and the beam fell on his face. Maxim quickly stood up. His knee hurt a bit after his fall, but it was nothing, because he had at once realized that it was Venka from the orchestra, with his light forelock amusingly standing on end when he clashed his cymbals. Scrawny, big-eyed Vladik resembled him because he was his younger brother.

"It's you!" said Maxim laughing joyfully.

"Oh, it's you!" responded Venka with a grin. "I guessed at once, when they told me that your name was Maxim...."

What else could be said? Everything was good: his new friends, the wind, the grass and the bright beam of the torch. And a shining moon over the mast and the trembling sail.

Maxim said:

"Do you know, I've bought an elephant, and it told me to feed him with toffees."

Venka did not reply, "Everybody says...."

He was glad. He said:

"Lucky day!"

The end

1976

Printed in Great Britain
by Amazon